EVERY SPIRITUAL BLESSING

by

Ken Hemphill

Auxano Press

Tigerville, South Carolina

ISBN 978-1-4944-4305-4

Published by Auxano Press
Tigerville, South Carolina
www.AuxanoPress.com

Dedicated to
Emerson Cadden Oswald
My granddaughter
And a Vivacious Young Lady with
A Passion for Learning.
With a Papa's prayer that you experience
And express Every Spiritual Blessing

Favorite Verse
Eph. 4:32 [And] be kind to one another,
compassionate, forgiving one another as God has
forgiven you in Christ.

CONTENTS

ACKNOWLEDGEMENTS

I am grateful to all the people at Auxano Press who work to ensure the accuracy, beauty, and serviceability of the non-disposable curricula. I am also grateful to a mom and dad, now in glory, who taught me to love and challenged me to study God's Word. I am indebted to many fine professors who challenged me to dig deep and rightly divide the Word of Truth. No one had a greater impact than the late Professor C.F.D. Moule, who led me through a dissertation which included a study of the book of Ephesians.

Paula, my wife and partner in ministry, continues to be my primary sounding board. She has had to endure hearing this material repeated in many settings as sermons before they ever became chapters in this book. She has a passion for the Word and the World which you will see reflected in all my writing. My children and their children continue to encourage me in my ministry of writing. In one sense, I have been passionate to write because I want my grandchildren and their generation to love God's Word and God's Church as much as their Nana and Papa do. I have thus decided to dedicate nine books in this series to my grandchildren. God's Redemption Story: Old Testament Survey was dedicated to my oldest granddaughter, Lois. This volume is dedicated to Emerson, our second grandchild.

Tina is our oldest daughter. She and her husband Brett Boesch have three children—Lois, Micah, and Naomi. Rachael Oswald and Trey are the parents of Emerson, Ward, and Ruby. Katie, the youngest, is married to Daniel Banks. They have three girls—Aubrey, Sloane, and Edie. These grandchildren bring us much joy and great hope. I pray that my books may offer them some encouragement as they come to know Christ and grow to serve Him.

I want to thank Dr. Jimmy Epting and the fine faculty and staff at North Greenville University for the privilege of serving as the founding director of the Center for Church Planting and Revitalization. The development of non-disposable curricula is one facet of North Greenville's strategy to assist local churches in healthy and biblical church growth. It is our conviction that nothing changes the heart and mind but the Word of God applied by the Spirit of God.

INTRODUCTION

I deeply love all of God's Word, but I must confess that I have a special place in my heart for the book of Ephesians. When Auxano Press undertook the project to provide sound biblical material for small group Bible study, I volunteered to write on Ephesians.

The book of Acts makes it abundantly clear that Paul had a special relationship with the church at Ephesus. Paul's last visit to Ephesus is both poignant and moving. He is on his way to Jerusalem with the calm assurance that bonds and affliction await him (Acts. 20:23). He is confident that he will never see his friends in Ephesus again this side of eternity. The final scene as described by Luke: "When he had said these things, he knelt down and prayed with them all. And they began to weep aloud and embraced Paul, and re-peatedly kissed him, grieving especially over the word which he had spoken, that they would not see his face again. And they were accompanying him to the ship" (Acts 20:36-38).

The letter itself reflects the same tender relation-ship between Paul and this church as Paul gives us the unique privilege of placing our ear to the door of his prayer closet as he prays for the church. The language of the letter is effusive as Paul pours out his heart in praise and petition. The theme of the letter is found in chapter 1, verse 3 as Paul declares: "Blessed be the God and Father of our Lord Jesus Christ, who has blessed us with every spiritual blessing in the heavenly places in Christ." Spiritual blessings are not to be consumed but rather conveyed. They enable the church to express

God's fullness (*pleroma*) in the world as Christ did in His incarnation. Ephesians is one of the most profound and challenging books of the New Testament. As you study it, whether alone or with your small group, I pray you will embrace and express all the spiritual blessings made available to you in Christ.

This book is part of the non-disposable curriculum from Auxano Press. As such, each chapter is designed to stand alone, but when taken together they will provide an exegetical study of the book of Ephesians. Free teaching guides are available online from auxanopress.com. If you want additional teaching helps, an audio commentary by the author and "Questions" by Josh Hunt are available at a reasonable cost. We believe the materials offer exceptional value to the church. We always appreciate your feedback. You can communicate with us either through our website, auxanopress.com or our Facebook page.

If you develop materials that could be helpful to other teachers, such as powerpoint presentations or teaching outlines, please feel free to submit them to us for possible inclusion as free resources.

For the sake of simplicity and brevity, footnotes are kept to a minimum in the entire series of books. I have profited greatly from many fine commentaries. Much of the research for this volume comes from my earlier works, *You Are Gifted: Your Spiritual Gifts and the Kingdom of God*, and *Connected Community: Becoming Family Through Church*.

Every Spiritual Blessing

Focal Text: Ephesians 1:1–14

I must begin this study with a personal confession. Ephesians is my favorite New Testament letter. It not only lays out the wonderful truth of the blessings available to all believers, but it places them in the context of our relationship to the church. Some people view "church" as an outdated and unnecessary encumbrance. But such is not the view expressed in this letter. The resurrection and exaltation of Christ are uniquely and inextricably bound to the empowering of the church, which is declared to be Christ's body on earth and "the fullness of Him who fills all in all" (1:23).

Paul wrote Ephesians, Colossians, and Philemon from prison. Epaphras, a leader of the church in Colossae (Col. 1:7; 4:12), visited Paul, bearing disturbing news about heretical teachings which devalued the person and work of Christ. Paul wrote Colossians to deal pointedly with these heretical teachings. He then penned Ephesians to undergird the ministry of the churches throughout Proconsular Asia. The bottom line of Ephesians is simple but profound: if Christ is not uniquely the Son of God, the church is nothing more than a spiritual country club. Yet, when we affirm the uniqueness of Christ, we must also affirm the significance of the church as His earthly body.

Salutation (1:1–2)

All of Paul's letters begin similarly—a mention of the writer, then the readers, followed by a word of

1

greeting. Although Paul's salutation follows the standard letter-writing style of his day, Paul lifts the greeting to a whole new level by describing both writer and recipient from the standpoint of their relationship to God. "Apostle" is a title Paul frequently uses to refer to himself. The word means someone acting as a fully authoritative representative of another. Paul was an apostle of Christ Jesus.

Paul calls his recipients "saints," a word which must be understood against the background of the Old Testament. In the Old Testament the tabernacle, the temple and its implements, and the people of Israel were "sanctified" or "set apart for God's service." As instruments in service to holy God, we are called to live in holiness. Did you know that the moment you were saved, you were set apart for kingdom service? Further, Paul describes the readers as "faithful," which carries the double meaning of persons who have faith and thus live faithfully.

Don't overlook the phrase "in Christ Jesus," which virtually sums up Paul's understanding of the Christian life. This phrase or an equivalent will be used eleven times in the first fourteen verses. We have faith in Him. All of God's blessings are found in Him. Our earthly existence has been lifted above this present world by our life in Him (cf. Col.3:1–3). Thus believers will find all needs met and all desires fulfilled "in Christ"—no other place and no other source. Notice that "saints" is plural, indicating that our sufficiency is "in Christ" but experienced corporately through His body, the church.

The Blessings of Redemption (1:3–12)

Paul begins his letter to the saints by a celebration of praise for God, the benefactor who provides "every spiritual blessing in the heavenly places in Christ" (1:3). In the New Testament "blessed" is only used of God. He alone is worthy to be blessed. Therefore, humankind is blessed only when we receive His blessing. Verses 3–13 form one long sentence in which the thought of one glorious blessing naturally leads to the contemplation of the next. The word "blessing" is singular, suggesting that a continuous flow of blessing comes from God. Like light reflected through a prism, the blessing of God takes on a rainbow of colors expressing the multifaceted beauty of His grace. The word "every" reflects the perfection of God's blessing. What do we possess "in Christ"? Every spiritual blessing! What do we lack? Nothing!

Before we consider individual blessings, we should pause and underline several truths that undergird the entire discussion: (1) Every spiritual blessing is in the heavenly places and therefore only accessible to those who are "in Christ." (2) From eternity God is at work accomplishing His will. (3) God's purpose is fulfilled in Christ. (4) Our intended purpose is to live "to the praise of His glory" (1:12). (5) Each person must hear and respond to the gospel to be sealed "in Him" (1:13).

Chosen to Be Holy and Blameless (v. 4)

God's plan of redemption existed before the foundation of the world. We refer to this as the doctrine of election, a concept that runs throughout the Bible. The beautiful doctrine of election is often misunderstood as if God is cold and calculating, predetermining who can be saved. What is determined before the foundation of the world is not the "who" of election but the "how" of election. We are chosen "in Him" where all the blessings of redemption reside. The key to understanding the two equal but seemingly contradictory truths of divine sovereignty and free will is the phrase "in Him." Since all the blessings of redemption are "in Him," we must ask how sinful man can come to be "in Christ." This question will be answered in verse 13.

Why does Paul begin the enumeration of blessings with an emphasis on God's choice of us "in Christ?" First, he establishes that God's redemptive activity began before time. It is a profound and humbling mystery to think that God planned to send His only begotten Son for our redemption before He created the world. Second, Paul wants us to understand that the end result of our chosenness is that we should be holy and blameless before Him. "Holy and blameless" harks back to the Old Testament sacrifice where only a perfect animal could be offered to God (Lev. 1:3). Now under grace we can offer ourselves to God with the full assurance that we are an acceptable sacrifice (cf. Rom. 12:1–2).

Predestined to Be Adopted as Sons (v. 5)

The phrase "in love" begins this thought, underlining the intimacy of the relationship between people and God. The word "predestined" means "marked out beforehand" and is simply another way to express the wonderful truth that God's plan for the adoption of fallen man was established before time began. From eternity past, God determined to adopt us as sons "through Jesus Christ to Himself."

Humans were created for fellowship with God. Sin led to the forfeiture of the intimate fellowship of sonship. Now by the grace of God and through the death of Christ, restoration to sonship is available. Adoption is a wonderful way to describe this newfound relationship because an adopted child has his position in the family by grace and not by birthright. Paul, born a Jew, celebrates His newfound relationship with God by crying out "Abba! Father!" because he has been adopted as a son (Rom. 8:15). God provided the means of adoption "according to the kind intention of His will."

In verse 6 we encounter the first of three occurrences of the phrase "to the praise of the glory of His grace." It is like the refrain to a glorious hymn. God's glory is the manifestation of His nature, and "grace" is a supreme manifestation of that nature. God's chosen people were called to live so as to bring praise to Him. Listen to Isaiah 43:21: "The people whom I formed for Myself will declare My praise." Now all persons who have received adoption through Christ and are thus "in Christ" are able to show forth the Father's nature and glorify Him. Grace, the unmerited favor of God, is only experienced "in the Beloved."

Redemption—the Forgiveness of Our Sins (vv. 7–8b)

The basic idea of redemption is "setting free" or "buying back." In the Old Testament provisions were made for redeeming land that had passed from an original owner to another. The people of Israel were redeemed from bondage in Egypt (Exod. 15:13, 19).

One of the most beautiful stories of redemption in the Old Testament is that of Hosea, who buys back his wife who has been enslaved by her own adultery.

Our redemption came at great expense—"through his blood." Once again we are led to think of the Old Testament sacrifices, particularly the Passover. The Jewish people understood that sin could not be set aside lightly. Sin created an objective problem that required a costly solution: "Without shedding of blood there is no forgiveness" (Heb. 9:22). What Old Testament sacrifices could not accomplish, Christ did through His own sacrificial death. The means of our redemption was also the cost of redemption.

Since man is a sinner by nature and by practice, redemption requires "forgiveness." Sin involves bondage, which includes the mind, the will, and even the members of our physical body. Forgiveness means the loosing of a person from that which binds him or her. Don't miss the last phrase—"according to the riches of His grace which He lavished on us." Forgiveness is not meted out in small portions with strings attached but is available in lavish abundance.

The Knowledge of the Mystery of His Will (vv. 8b–10)

The blessings of redemption continue to build one upon the other. Those whom God redeems, He enlightens with the understanding of His kingdom purpose and their role in it. Paul will return to this theme in chapters 2 and 3, so we will only touch on this wonderful truth now. The combination of "wisdom and insight" indicates that we receive knowledge that leads to transformation. Ours is not simply a higher intellectual knowledge but the life-changing understanding of God's purpose in the world and our role in it (see Eph. 3:8–10).

The word "mystery" conveys the idea of something that can be comprehended only when it is revealed. Paul's mystery is different from the strange and baseless heathen mystery religions popular in Proconsular Asia. "Mystery" here is the truth of God in Christ, given to the church to declare to the world and revealed to all who would respond.

The revelation of this mystery flowed from the kindness of God. Not only does Christ provide the way for a sinful person to enter into fellowship with God, but He is the means whereby God will bring unity to the whole universe, disordered by man's rebellion and sin. The word "administration" speaks of the full government of all things for God's people. The word translated "times" comes from a Greek word which speaks of decisive moments in the fulfillment of the purposes of God. Through His activity in history, God will one day restore and unify everything, material and spiritual, under Christ's headship. This verse does not teach universal salvation but universal domination under one head.

A Predestined Inheritance—the Praise of His Glory (vv. 11–12)

Persons "in Him" have a promised inheritance. In Christ we have been admitted to the ranks of His holy people, and thus we have an undeserved but rich inheritance. Our inheritance now and forever is that we will show forth the glory of God. We are able to show the world God's glory by manifesting His character through our lives as we are transformed from glory to glory (2 Cor. 3:18). One day in heaven we will fully reflect His glory in His presence. Are you displaying God's glory through your daily actions?

Paul has already used the word "predestined" in verse 5 to speak of God's eternal plan to adopt us as sons. Here he uses it to speak of God's plan to bring the redeemed—Jew and Gentile, male and female—into a community which would be His own possession. Again, predestination refers to "what" and not "who". Whatever God declares, He accomplishes since He "works all things after the counsel of His will." No power in heaven or on earth can stop God from fulfilling His predestined plan to make all those "in Christ" His own heritage.

In Him (1:13–14)

Verse 13 begins with the phrase "in Him" because it raises and answers the question of how sinful man can come to be "in Him." "You also" may speak specifically of Gentiles since Paul spoke of the Jews in verse 12 as those "who were first to hope in Christ." Jews and Gentiles now have the same access to God as they listen to the gospel and believe. The gospel is here described as "the message of truth"—that is, the revelation of God in Christ (Eph. 4:21).

Let's take a moment and lay out the steps necessary for one to be "in Him" and receive all the blessings predestined for those "in Christ": (1) Listen to the message of the truth. (2) Believe the message. Hearing is vain unless it leads to faith which enables man to respond. (3) After listening and believing, we are sealed in Him with the Holy Spirit of promise.

In the ancient world a seal was a personal sign of an owner that distinguished true from false. It was also the guarantee that the item delivered had, in fact, arrived intact. The unmistakable mark of the believer is the activity of the Spirit who bears witness with our spirit and produces fruit and gifts in our lives empowering us for ministry. The Spirit is the "pledge" or "down payment" who assures that our ultimate and total redemption as God's possession will result in the praise of His glory. Talk about secure forever!

FOR MEMORY AND MEDITATION

"Blessed be the God and Father of our Lord Jesus Christ, who has blessed us with every spiritual blessing in the heavenly places in Christ." Ephesians 1:3

Prayer for Enlightenment

Focal Text: Ephesians 1:15–23

In many of his letters, Paul indicates that he has been constantly praying for the church. Wouldn't you like to have had the opportunity to put your ear to the door of Paul's prayer closet as he interceded on behalf of his churches? Ephesians gives us an opportunity to do just that.

Paul's Prayer Strategy (1:15–17)

We often overlook little connecting phrases in the Scripture, but each word inspired by the Holy Spirit is intentional and therefore important. This section begins with the little phrase "for this reason." This phrase links Paul's passionate prayer with all that has gone before. Because followers of Christ have received such abundant blessing and have such incredible kingdom potential, Paul prays that his readers might fully comprehend and embrace all available resources.

Paul indicates that his prayers have been prompted by reports he has heard concerning their "faith in the Lord Jesus." The fact that he has only "heard" of the faith of some of his recipients indicates that this letter was intended for distribution beyond the church at Ephesus. The term "at Ephesus" in verse 2 may simply indicate where the letter began its journey as it made its way to the other churches of Proconsular Asia. The seven churches, listed together in Revelation, may have functioned like a modern-day association of churches who supported and encouraged one another. This letter likely was originally intended for all seven of these churches.

The phrase "faith in the Lord Jesus which exists among you" is a direct reference to the conversion of the recipients through the preaching of the gospel. Their "love for all the saints" was clear and indisputable evidence of the authenticity of their faith. True conversion not only impacts one's relationship to God; it also alters one's relationship to others, and especially to other members of the household of faith. We are "born again" into a family of believers that spans the globe, has no racial or social barriers, and lasts for all eternity. When we fall deeply in love with Christ, we will express that love in relationship with "all the saints."

The underlying passion of Paul's prayer is defined by the request that God would give to believers "a spirit of wisdom and of revelation in the knowledge of Him" (v. 17). "Spirit" here refers to the human spirit informed by the Holy Spirit. The word "wisdom" is listed first because the truths of the gospel, accessible only by revelation, are so overwhelming and wonderful it is impossible for humans to comprehend them unless they are willing to be taught by God. Paul is not praying that believers would acquire more knowledge of certain truths about God but that they would grow in the "knowledge of Him." We can know about God and yet not know God. Personal knowledge of God always leads to life in union and fellowship with God.

The one who hears and responds to believers' prayers is described as "the God of our Lord Jesus Christ, the Father of glory." This phrase indicates that the one true God is the God whom Jesus both acknowledges as God and reveals to us. Jesus readily spoke of the Father as "my God" (Matt. 27:46; John 20:17). This phrase in no way suggests that Jesus is less than God. The one true God is the Father to whom all glory belongs.

The Threefold Request (1:18–23)

The prayer begins with a plea that "the eyes of your heart may be enlightened." Man without God is darkened in his understanding and thus behaves according to the futility of his mind (Eph. 4:17–18). Believers, however, are renewed in the spirit of their mind (4:23). The "heart" is not simply the seat of emotions or the intellect, but it is the center of one's personality. We might say "heart" stands for the inner man in his entirety, the seat of intelligence and will. Thus Paul is not simply praying for "head" knowledge which informs, but a "heart" knowledge which transforms. With the goal of transformation in mind, Paul prays they will know three things that are staggering in their breadth.

The Hope of His Calling (v. 18)

The calling of God speaks of God's choice of His people "in Christ" before the foundation of the world. As we have seen, this calling is made effective as persons respond to God's call freely presented through the gospel of salvation (1:13). God's calling speaks first of His initiative in salvation as His Holy Spirit convicts of sin and brings individuals to Christ. In terms of redemption, God's calling to salvation was a past-tense reality for the recipients of this letter. God's calling always has a present-tense context as He calls believers to a lifelong vocation of service. Calling to salvation is inextricably bound with the calling to join God in His kingdom mission. But since our calling comes from an eternal God, it brings us expectation and hope for an eternal destiny.

The Riches of the Glory of His Inheritance in the Saints (v. 18)

As you read this phrase aloud, notice its striking beauty. Commentators differ on whether this verse speaks of the believers' inheritance or of believers being God's inheritance. The hope of God's calling certainly involves a rich inheritance for God's people, as Paul has already enumerated in the first twelve verses where he discussed "every spiritual blessing" which is in Christ. Nevertheless, Paul has also indicated that believers are God's own possession or inheritance (1:14). God has determined to display His manifold wisdom to the entire universe through His people (3:10). In Old Testament times God considered Israel to be His unique possession through which He desired to manifest His name so the nations would be drawn to Him. That privilege and responsibility are now applied to those Paul addresses as "saints" (1:2, 18). In other words, we are God's heritage—His own possession through whom He will bring glory to Himself by accomplishing His kingdom agenda.

Have you ever contemplated the truth that God considers you the glory of His inheritance? Readers who have children or grandchildren certainly understand what it means to speak of them as our heritage. We know the pleasure it gives us to see them embody our values and succeed in life. F. F. Bruce writes, "We can scarcely realize what it must mean to God to see His purpose complete, to see creatures of His hand, sinners redeemed by His grace, reflecting His own glory."[1] God has determined to advance His kingdom on earth and thus manifest His glory through His community of born-again believers who have been set aside for His purposes—His church. We must continually ask ourselves, "Are we reflecting His glory by advancing His kingdom?"

The Surpassing Greatness of His Power toward Us Who Believe (1:19–23)

Since our calling and commission are of such great consequence, Paul prays for an understanding of the vast power "toward us who believe." This odd-sounding phrase means "the power available to us and working through us." So great is our need of supernatural empowering that Paul will use six verses and exhaust the Greek vocabulary to convey something of the character of the power made available to His church.

The phrase "in accordance with the working of the strength of His might" makes clear that we are contemplating nothing less than supernatural empowering. When we think of supernatural power, we may think of Old Testament events such as the opening of the Red Sea, but nothing can exceed the demonstration of power which Paul brings to the table—the resurrection and exaltation of Christ.

Paul finds Greek words such as *dunamis* (power), *energeia* (working), *kratos* (strength), and *ischys* (might) inadequate for explaining the power made available through the resurrection. He modifies the description of power by the use of a participle translated here as "surpassing greatness." Paul alone uses this participle. He uses it twice in 2 Corinthians, once to describe the surpassing glory of the new covenant (3:10) and a second time to indicate that the generosity of giving was evidence of the "surpassing grace of God" (9:14) working through the Corinthians. The only other uses are in Ephesians. In 2:7 he writes of the "surpassing riches of His grace" that God will show us in the ages to come, and in 3:19 he writes of the love of Christ which "surpasses knowledge." The power available to His church surpasses description!

Paul now moves to the one supreme event that demonstrates the power "toward us." Ours is the power that raised Jesus from the dead and seated Him at the right hand of the Father. The raising of the Son demonstrates the Father's approval (Acts 4:10), affirms Jesus as the Son (Acts 17:31), and declares Him to be Lord of all (Rom. 1:4). While the cross may be the supreme demonstration of the love of God (Rom. 5:8), the resurrection is the demonstration of the power of God.

We have already encountered the phrase "the heavenly places" in verse 3 as Paul discussed the spiritual blessings available to believers who are "in Christ," who now sits enthroned "in the heavenly places." The ascension of Christ is a clear declaration of His power to forgive sin (Heb. 1:3; 1 Pet. 3:21–22) and to keep His followers secure for all eternity (Col. 3:1–4). The "heavenly places" is where He makes intercession for believers (Rom. 8:34). The reference to God's right hand is not to be understood in a spatial sense, but in terms of power and authority by which the exalted and rightful King administers the government of heaven and earth. Paul alludes to Psalm 110:1; "The LORD says to my Lord; 'Sit at My right hand until I make Your enemies a footstool for Your feet.' " This verse, related to the anointing of the King of Israel, has it's supreme and ultimate fulfillment in the ascension of Christ.

Paul elaborates on the subjection of all other powers and authorities by stating it both positively and negatively. In verse 21, he focuses on the exaltation of the Christ, and in verse 22 he draws attention to the subjection of all things to Christ. While it is possible that terms like "rule," "authority," "power," and "dominion" may have some application to the powers venerated by the false teachers of Paul's day, Paul is unconcerned to delineate between them. Whatever powers may exist in the seen or unseen world, in this age or the age to come, one thing is certain—Christ is sovereign over them. His authority is totally comprehensive. The only difference between this age and the age to come will be the open and total manifestation of that power. The world rulers of darkness, mentioned in Ephesians 6:12, exercise some control in the present age through deceit and darkness, but in the coming age that will be a thing of the past.

Verse 22 restates and summarizes all that has been said with a reference to Psalm 8:6, which speaks of God's original plan for man's dominion over creation: "You made him to rule over the works of Your hands; You have put all things under his feet." Man, through sin, lost this position of dominion over God's creation. Only one new and true Man, Christ Jesus, fulfilled God's divine purpose. Now through Him and in Him we are restored to our true dignity and purpose.

Paul concludes by declaring that all of this has been accomplished for the church, "which is His body, the fullness of Him who fills all in all." Christ, as Lord over all things, is by supreme appointment head of the church. In this case "head" not only speaks of authority but also to the vital unity between Christ and the church. This unity is further emphasized by the phrase "which is His body." This is the first occurrence of the word "church" in this letter. It calls to mind the "community" or "assembly" of the people of God in the Old Testament. The Lord Himself changed the scope of this word when He declared His intention of building His church (Matt. 16:18). The church was envisioned by God before creation; it is continuous with the people of God in Old Testament era, but it is new in Christ.

The church as "body" is unique to Paul. It signifies the living power which unites the people of God to Christ and one another. The life and power of the risen Christ flows through His church, and thus each of us and all of us must function in obedience to Him to carry out His mission in the world. The church is empowered to be the full expression of Christ who is Himself the full expression of God (Col. 1:19). This is a major theme of this letter. The idea that the church can fully express Christ is not simply a beautiful ideal; it is both the potential and the purpose of the church.

Since the power of the resurrection has been made available to His church, why do we attempt and accomplish so little with so much at stake?

For Memory and Meditation

"And He put all things in subjection under His feet, and gave Him as head over all things to the church, which is His body, the fullness of Him who fills all in all." Ephesians 1:22–23

---

[1] F. F. Bruce, *The Epistle to the Ephesians* (London: Pickering & Inglis, 1961), 40.

Alive Together With Christ

CHAPTER 3

Focal Text: Ephesians 2:1–10

If you have ever participated in any form of witness training, you may have been asked to write your personal testimony based on the initials BC, RC, and AC. In case you missed that class, BC stands for "before Christ," RC stands for "receiving Christ," and AC stands for "after Christ." You were to tell what your life was like before you received Christ, to explain how you came to know Christ, and then to tell what has changed since you received Christ. If you have never written your personal story, it is a great idea, and this section may give you a few pointers. Paul follows this outline as he writes about God's great love and mercy which led to our redemption.

Life Before Christ (2:1–3)

Some of us have been saved so long, or we were saved at such a young age, that we have forgotten what life was like before Christ. Paul's discussion of grace is set against the backdrop of the universal sinfulness of man and the hopelessness of his situation. The opening phrase, "and you were dead" delivers the knockout punch. A dead man cannot accomplish any meritorious deeds which he might claim in his own defense. With respect to man's spiritual nature, he is dead in trespasses and sins.

"Trespasses" express the idea of "missing the mark," while "sins" indicates "slipping from the way." Both words express our failure to live as we should. Man was created in God's image and designed to live in His presence. In the creation narrative we see a picture of God's original plan for humankind. Freedom was given to man but with a warning that it entailed the possibility of disobedience which would lead to death (Gen. 2:17). Adam and Eve discovered that death was not, in the first instance, physical death—no, it was much worse than that. It was the loss of the spiritual life which allowed man to live in perfect fellowship with God. Thus "dead in your trespasses and sins" accurately describes man's condition before life in Christ.

Beginning in verse 2, we find a hint of good news concerning the recipients of this letter. Notice the repetition of "formerly" in verses 2 and 3. Paul is writing to believers, and thus they can celebrate that they are no longer dead in sin. Verse 2 focuses on the plight of Gentiles, but the "we too" in verse 3 includes the Jews. Sin and the resulting spiritual death are the plight of all mankind.

Paul uses the common image of walking here to speak of the conduct of one's life (cf. Mark 7:5; Acts 21:21). In Ephesians 4:17, Paul uses this imagery to speak of Gentile or pagan behavior. In the present context Paul explains the walk of the dead man by two phrases introduced by the word "according." First, he/she is walking "according to the course of this world." Paul means the world in rebellion against God. The man who is spiritually dead is controlled by earthbound motives and desires and has no regard for the kingship of Christ. He lives without any realization of God's presence—he has no Godward activity. Fallen man's goals and desires are based on values established by a world that is already in the process of decay.

Further, dead men walk "according to the prince of the power of the air." The devil is the leader of the spiritual hosts of wickedness in the heavenly places (cf. Eph. 6:12). Believers are set free from bondage to him based on the victory of Christ (Col. 2:15), but unbelievers are still subject to the devil and live with his God-denying goals. Paul describes the condition of the unsaved as being under the control of the "spirit that is now working in the sons of disobedience." The idea is that anyone not controlled by the Spirit of God is subject to the energizing (working) of the spirit which has the evil one as its source.

No doubt many non-Christians would recoil at this description of their life. They would argue that they are self-made and self-controlled. They would be offended by the suggestion that their life is under the control of the devil, who they may view as a figure of ancient mythology. Such is the subtlety of his plan and power. He gladly lets men believe he doesn't exist as long as he convinces them that God doesn't either. As long as man lives "according to the course of this world," Satan's plan is working.

In verse 3 Paul switches to the first-person plural to include himself along with all Jews. Many religious Jews of the first century would have readily agreed that verses 1–2 described the condition of the Gentiles. Paul makes clear that the sin problem is universal. "We too" once "lived in the lusts of our flesh, indulging the desires of the flesh and of the mind." When we read "desires of the flesh," we often think of sins of a sexual or material nature. But sins of the flesh can be seemingly harmless things like those Paul listed in Philippians 3:4–6, which were also the manifestation of his "confidence in the flesh." Simply put, the unregenerate nature of man can manifest itself in respectable and prideful ways as well as despicable ones. Dead men live a self-centered life rather than a God-centered one.

The fall of man impacts his total being—the entire reasoning process (cf. Col. 1:21). The word translated "mind" is actually plural and could be translated "thoughts." Without the renewal of the mind (Rom. 12:1–2), our thoughts are on earthly fulfillment and self-gratification.

What does Paul mean when he says that we are "children of wrath"? Some have mistakenly taken this phrase to mean that we are born with a nature that makes us subject to the wrath of God even before we sin. Such an interpretation goes beyond the doctrine of "original sin" to one of "original guilt," a concept not taught in the Bible. "Children" here refers to people of a certain "type" without any reference to what they have inherited from their parents. For example, in Ephesians 2:2, Paul speaks of "children of disobedience" and in Ephesians 5:8 to "children of light." Both are addressed to the same recipients, and neither condition was based on inheritance from their parents but upon their own volition. Paul elaborates more fully on man's sin nature in Romans 1:18–2:29. Man's sin problem is related both to his fallen nature and to his decision to sin, which makes him both responsible and culpable.[1]

These opening verses paint a dark and depressing picture of man's spiritual condition apart from Christ.

It provides the canvas on which Paul can paint, in the most vivid colors, the riches of God's mercy and the greatness of His love.

But God, Being Rich in Mercy (2:4–7)

I love the phrase "but God." My good friend Karolyn Chapman, the accomplished and vivacious wife of Dr. Gary Chapman, challenged me to write a little devotional book by that title. You will be surprised to find the number of occasions in the Bible when "but God" is used to signal the in-breaking of the grace and power of God.

God's loving action on behalf of fallen man issued from His mercy. God expressed His love "even when we were dead in our transgressions" (2:5). God's love led to the ultimate sacrifice of His only begotten Son (John 3:16) while man was in rebellion against Him and thus unworthy and undeserving of such love. Because of His love believers are no longer exposed to God's wrath.

Out of death came life! The Greek verb translated "made us alive together" may be a word Paul coined to express how sinful man has been joined to Christ through God's redemptive activity. It only occurs here and in Colossians 2:13 to express the believers' union with Christ in His death and resurrection. It may also express a truth which will be more fully developed in the second half of this chapter—the union of all believers, whether Jew or Gentile, in Christ. The possibility of new life for men dead in transgressions necessitated the death and resurrection of the new man, Christ. Jesus, in His death, suffered the consequences of sin and thus removed the barrier to fellowship with God caused by man's sin. His resurrection demonstrated His triumph over physical and spiritual death. By listening and responding to the gospel, we can be sealed in Him (1:13) and have new life.

While Paul will discuss salvation by grace in more detail in verses 8–9, he simply cannot restrain himself from adding his favorite summation of the gospel at this point (v. 5b). Redemption is based solely on God's grace, His unmerited favor. The perfect tense of the verb used here indicates a completed action with a continuing result. Our redemption is a deliverance from the penalty of sin, the power of sin, and ultimately the presence of sin.

Verse 6 is pivotal, serving as somewhat of a summary of the letter. We were first introduced to the spiritual blessing in the heavenly places in 1:3. Later in 1:20, Paul talked about the display of power when God raised His Son and seated Him in the heavenly places. Now he declares a truth so glorious it is virtually inexplicable. God has "raised us up with Him, and seated us with Him in the heavenly places in Christ Jesus." The verbs translated "made alive, raised up, and seated" are all in the aorist tense, indicating what has already been accomplished on our behalf. Our citizenship has been transferred to heaven (Phil. 3:20). Temporarily we remain in our earthly bodies and are constrained to this earth, but "in Christ" we are already seated in the heavenly places with Christ.

Don't miss the little connecting phrase "so that" in verse 7. His purpose is to show or display to us and through us "the surpassing riches of His grace in kindness toward us in Christ Jesus." In the eternal future, as age succeeds age, the bounty of God's grace will be

seen as He
Paul used
of the c
power
that '
wit'
T

His redeemed family.
J *huperbalon* to speak
nonstration of God's
he same word to assert
—His church—together
monstration of His mercy.
e church is lifted beyond
nity as it displays God's
nd the world (cf. 3:10).

ed on God's initiative and activ-
qualifying phrases to underline
grace: "not of yourselves," "gift of
esult of works." Since dead men
hemselves, they have no basis for

boa.

Man   the entire drama of redemption can be expressed with two simple words—"through faith" (cf. Rom. 3:22–24 and Gal. 3:16). Some have misinterpreted this verse, suggesting that Paul is saying "faith" is the gift of God, and thus man has no role in salvation since "responding faith" is a gift of God for some and not for others. The demonstrative pronoun "that" is neuter whereas "faith" is a feminine noun, indicating that the entire process of "salvation by grace through faith" is the gift of God.

The entire initiative and every part of making Salvation available to sinful man are God's alone. The mercy of God and the work of God made redemption possible. The voice of God awakens man to his need. The Spirit of God prompts man to respond to the gospel, but man must still respond in faith. Our faith does

27

nothing that merits salvation; it is simply the faculty by which man must accept the salvation God's grace has made possible in Christ.

Salvation is "not a result of works" because it is given by grace, and as a gift man must receive it by faith. Men of every age and of every religion have been tempted to think their lives are good enough to merit salvation. Nothing could be further from the truth; else the sacrifice of God's Son was unnecessary and cruel.

His Workmanship (2:10)

While we are not saved by good works, we are most assuredly saved for good works. The word translated "workmanship" indicates that we are God's masterpiece. Man, created in God's image, was the zenith of God's original creation. That image was marred by man's sin and rebellion. But those in Christ are now part of His new creation. We have been newly designed for "good works," which declare that we are His workmanship. The preposition "for" indicates that "good works" and new life are inseparable. The foreknowledge of an omniscient God is not opposed to His gift of free will and responsibility. We must choose to accomplish the good works God has prepared for us.

FOR MEMORY AND MEDITATION

"For we are His workmanship, created in Christ Jesus for good works, which God prepared beforehand, so that we would walk in them." Ephesians 2:10

---

1 This discussion is a summary of that given by Francis Foulkes, *Ephesians* (London: Tyndale Press, 1963), 71.

He Himself Is Our Peace

CHAPTER 4

Focal Text: Ephesians 2:11–22

The desire and hope for peace and reconciliation continue unabated from people to people and from century to century, but divisions and conflicts still abound. I attended university during the Vietnam conflict, and I can still recall the protests of the war and the cries for peace. Often those "peaceful demonstrations" actually resulted in conflict. It made one wonder if there was any real possibility that lasting and meaningful peace could be established between peoples in conflict.

Paul was a rigorous and proud Jew who grew up looking down on the Gentiles. Many Jews referred to them as "dogs"—not the cuddly house pet variety but the vicious street pack variety. Contact with a Gentile could render a Jew unclean. The barrier between Jews and Gentiles had racial, cultural, and religious overtones. It was symbolized by the wall which separated the court of the Gentiles from the temple proper which was posted with signs in multiple languages forbidding entry to Gentiles upon threat of death. This wall of separation was one barrier which came tumbling down.

Remember You Were Once Excluded (2:11–12)

The connecting "therefore" makes clear that Paul is still discussing the impact of grace and what it means to be "His workmanship" (2:10). Twice Paul calls upon his readers to "remember" their former condition be-

29

fore the invasion of grace. God's grace is individually experienced, but it always has consequences which are corporate in nature. Personal redemption brings us into the community of the redeemed which is made up of people from all races and backgrounds. The church is God's workmanship (2:10) and thus the canvas on which He displays His manifold wisdom (3:10).

The Jews took great pride in the rite of circumcision as an outward sign of their covenant relationship with God. For Paul circumcision was irrelevant for the new order which had been brought about through faith in Christ (cf. Gal. 5:6; 6:15). It was an external mark that was "performed in the flesh by human hands" (v. 11) in contrast to the redemptive work of Christ which transformed the heart. The Jews, who had been chosen by God to join Him in His redemptive mission, should have shared the good things of God with the Gentiles; but they simply viewed them as uncircumcised pagans.

In verse 12 Paul paints the picture of lostness in the darkest tones possible. Listen to the words of exclusion—"separate," "excluded," "strangers," "no hope," "without God." The overarching issue for Paul is that all people were "separate from Christ." Since all the blessings of the heavenlies are in Christ (1:3), to be separated from Him is to fail to have life. The phrase "excluded from the commonwealth of Israel" was a reminder that Gentiles could only be admitted to the commonwealth of Israel as a proselyte, a difficult process which still left them little more than second-class citizens. "Covenants of promise" refers to the promises to Abraham and the patriarchs, which involved assurance of a coming

Messiah who would bring deliverance and future glory. Since Gentiles were excluded from the covenants, they were without hope and without God. This is actually an accurate description of the Gentile world of Jesus' day. The pantheon of gods worshipped by Greeks and Romans gave no hope.

"Without God" does not mean God had forsaken them or the Gentiles had rejected Him but rather that they had no real knowledge of God. This is true of much of the world today. Many people around the world and around your block have not rejected God; they simply have little or no true knowledge of Him.

But Now in Christ Jesus (2:13–18)

From the dark tones of separation, we move to the beautiful colors of inclusion. Everything changes with the phrase "but now in Christ Jesus." Those who were far off have brought near; those who were separated from the commonwealth and the covenants are now part of one new man.

The language of being "far off" and "brought near" echo the words of Isaiah 57:19b, which will be alluded to again in Ephesians 2:17. "Peace, peace to him who is far and to him who is near." Being brought near is not the timid approach of a proselyte to Judaism, but is something far more wonderful—peace with God through the "blood of Christ." The blood of Christ is His life willingly given on the cross as a sin offering. "Far off" refers to the Gentiles, while "near" refers to the Jews, God's covenant people. Since the cause of man's estrangement from God was not his nationality but his sin condition, both groups must be brought to God through the blood of Christ.

Christ is our peace individually and corporately. Those who enter into peace with God must of necessity live in peace with all His children. When Christ reconciles us to God, He breaks down all barriers that divide His children from one another. The dividing wall Paul had in mind was likely the wall between the courts of the Gentiles and the inner court where notices were posted warning Gentiles to keep out. Paul had personal knowledge of the power of this barrier. He was accused of taking a Gentile into the inner court, an accusation that led to his arrest and Roman imprisonment (Acts 21).

The physical wall in the temple stood as a powerful symbol of the issues that divided Jew from Gentile. The real barriers, however, were racial, religious, political, and cultural. No barrier we face today would be any greater than the enmity that existed between Jew and Gentile in the first century. Such long-standing and deeply ingrained divisions were not overcome by compromise or negotiation but by the single event of the cross where Christ abolished all the barriers that divide men.

The phrase "Law of commandments contained in ordinances" (v. 15) may refer to the elaborate system of legal observances which publicly marked Jew from Gentile, such as the regulations about food being clean and unclean. The Lord's death abolished all enmity by making Jew and Gentile into one new man. The one new man is the Christian community viewed corporately. Gentiles do not rise to the status of Jews, but both groups have become something new and greater.

"New" means that both groups have entered a quality of community which did not exist prior to the crucifixion and the resurrection.

Paul doesn't want to leave any doubt that reconciliation to God will necessarily result in reconciliation to man, and thus he underlines this truth with slightly different words in verse 16. When Christ was slain on the cross, He bore man's sins and thus put to death the enmity between sinful man and holy God. Reconciliation to God made possible the reconciliation of Jew and Gentile by bringing them together in one new body. Here "body" refers to the living organism in which diverse members belong together. The body is nothing less than the church, the family of the redeemed.

Paul fortifies his argument by citing the Old Testament, a citation which probably echoes both Isaiah 52:7 and 57:19. Both Gentiles (far away) and Jews (near) must hear and respond to the same message. Christ is the gospel of peace for all men since His cross provides the only access to the Father for sinful man. Both Jew and Gentile have "access in one Spirit to the Father" (v. 18). The peace and reconciliation Paul speaks of is not simply a truce which removes hostility; it positively brings Jews and Gentiles on common ground before God the Father. There is one Holy Spirit, whose work in the hearts of Jews and Gentiles alike gives them access to God and enables them to become children of God (Rom. 8:15). Can you think of areas of division in your church or community that need this message of peace?

You Are God's Household (2:19–22)

The apostle once again addresses the matter of the inclusion of the Gentile into the new community which was established by the sacrificial death of Christ. They are "no longer strangers and aliens," who might live alongside a people in their country but with only superficial rights. They are now "fellow citizens" and therefore have all the rights and privileges of citizenship. Roman citizenship was a prized possession and assured a person of unique rights and privileges. When Paul was accused and arrested for taking a Gentile into the inner court, he reminded the commander that he was a Roman citizen, which immediately impacted the way he was treated (Acts 21:39–40). Believers are not simply citizens; they are citizens with the saints. The term "saints" was often used to refer to Old Testament saints, but since Paul has already used it in the first verse of this epistle to refer to the believers at Ephesus, it likely means the same here.

"Citizenship" is limited in its ability to describe the intimacy of the new status available to the Gentiles, and thus Paul calls them members of "God's household." They are now full members of the family of God (cf. Heb. 3:6). In Romans 8:15–17 Paul spoke with wonder about the ability to address God as "Abba! Father!" His adoption as a son made him a child and an heir. Gentiles have the intimacy of relationship with God that can best be described as members of God's family.

Paul now uses a third image—holy temple—to speak of the mission of those who are citizens of heaven and members of God's family. We must never forget that redemption and mission are intertwined throughout Scripture. God blessed Abraham that he might in turn bless the nations (Gen. 12:1–3). After the Exodus, God commissioned Israel to join Him in reaching the nations as He declared them to be "a kingdom of priests" and "a holy nation" (Exod. 19:5–6).

The image of the building begins in verse 20 where Paul speaks first of the foundation of the apostles and prophets. Paul uses a similar image in 1 Corinthians 3 where Christ is declared to be the foundation of the building. There Paul speaks of the work of himself and Apollos and then reminds his readers that all believers must build on this foundation. He challenges readers to build with quality materials since each person's work will be tested.

The imagery here is slightly different from that of 1 Corinthians 3 since Christ is viewed as the cornerstone rather than the foundation, but the truths taught are certainly compatible. The foundation here is declared to be the "apostles and prophets," meaning the New Testament apostles and prophets (cf. 4:11). The church is based on a unique historical event with Christ at its center. The apostles and prophets, who by the Spirit bore witness to Christ, had a unique foundational role in the establishment of the church.

The idea of the cornerstone comes from Psalm 118:22 and Isaiah 28:16. Peter quotes both of these texts (1 Pet. 2:6–8) as prophetic references to the ministry of Christ. The cornerstone is cut out beforehand and, when placed in the foundation, serves to bond the structure together and demonstrate that the building has been carried out according to the specifications of the builder. All other stones find their alignment and usefulness only in relationship to the cornerstone. Have you considered the implications of this truth for your ministry and service through the church?

Since Paul is not speaking of a physical building, he slightly alters the image by using a biological verb "growing," which maintains the image of the church as a living organism. "In whom" refers to Christ who alone enables the church to grow. In Christ the entire building is "fitted together." The verb translated "being fitted together" occurs only once more in the New Testament, and that is in Ephesians 4:16 where Paul discusses how the gifted church functions for maximum growth.

Notice that the church "is growing," and its growth will not be complete until the Lord returns for His bride (Rev. 21). It is continually growing as it expands God's kingdom to the ends of the earth in preparation for His return. The reference to the "holy temple" reminds us of the Old Testament temple which served as a special meeting place between God and His people. It was the place where God's glory descended. When Christ came, the physical temple became obsolete since He was the temple not made with hands. His body expressed the glory of God and provided the place where man and God could meet (cf. John 1:12–14).

While the physical temple of Jesus' body is no longer among men, He is still present in the context of His holy people, His church. It is the place where God's glory will be manifest (3:10) and the message of His redemption declared.

Did you notice that verse 21 ends with the phrase "in the Lord" and verse 22 ends with "in the Spirit"?

Only as we abide in Christ and are empowered by the Holy Spirit are we able to participate in the supernatural work of building the church into a dwelling of God.

Too much is at stake for us to play church!

For Memory and Meditation

"So then you are no longer strangers and aliens, but you are fellow citizens with the saints, and are of God's household." Ephesians 2:19

The Mystery Hidden
for Ages

CHAPTER 5

Focal Text: Ephesians 3:1–13

Most people enjoy a good mystery. My wife has me record Masterpiece Theater that airs on the public broadcasting channel on Sunday nights. Whether the sleuth is Miss Marpel, Sherlock Holmes, or Inspector Poirot, we watch in rapt anticipation as the mystery is finally solved.

Paul uses the word "mystery" three times in this brief passage. He has already used the word in Ephesians 1:9, and in both contexts it means the truth of God revealed in Christ to all who will receive it. Paul may have repeatedly used the word "mystery" in this letter to draw an intentional contrast to the strange and baseless mystery cults so popular in the first century and the mystery which has been made known in Christ. For Paul the fundamental mystery, which had now been revealed, was the means by which God brings alienated man back into relationship with Himself and thus opens the possibility for restored unity for the whole universe—a unity which has been disrupted by man's sin and rebellion. Thus the word "mystery" means something "revealed" rather than something "mysterious." Not only has this mystery been revealed by God in Christ; it must now be proclaimed by the church to the whole world.

By Revelation, according to Grace (3:1–7)

Earlier in chapter 1 we noticed that Paul was so overwhelmed by the description of the blessings made available in Christ that he was moved to pray (15–23). Having just described the one new man made up of Jew and Gentile, (2:11–22) Paul is once again compelled to pray. As he begins to pray, he considers his own role in the unveiling of God's eternal plan for Jew and Gentile to become one new man and interrupts his prayer to speak, in humble gratitude, of his grace-empowered ministry.

Paul begins with a reference to his imprisonment "for the sake of you Gentiles" (3:1). He was likely thinking of the imprisonment recorded in Acts 21:17–34 when Paul was falsely accused of taking a Gentile into the inner court of the temple. This allegation caused Paul's Jewish opponents to respond with bitter hostility, which ultimately led to a trial by Roman authorities. Notice, however, that Paul did not consider himself to be a prisoner of Rome but of Christ and that on behalf of the Gentiles. His imprisonment had actually afforded him new opportunities to spread the gospel, and thus he seeks neither pity nor praise. He desires simply to encourage his readers, for his present tribulations are for their advantage (see 3:13).

The phrase "if . . . you have heard" is a bit surprising when one remembers the length of time Paul spent in Ephesus. We are once again reminded that this letter was to be shared with an audience beyond the church at Ephesus. Paul refers to his ministry as a "stewardship of God's grace" (3:2). Paul uses the word "stewardship" in Colossians 1:25 in reference to his ministry through the church. "Of this church I was made a minister according to the stewardship from God bestowed on me for your benefit, so that I might fully carry out the preaching of the word of God."

The word "grace" has a range of meanings in Pauline writings. It not only speaks of the grace we experience in redemption but also of the grace of calling and empowering for service. It is the unmerited favor of God which brings man to salvation and provides all he needs for the living of a meaningful Christian life (cf. 2 Cor. 9:8). In Ephesians 4:7 and Romans 12:3 and 6 Paul uses "grace" to speak of a particular task and the gifting to accomplish that task. Grace enabled Paul to lay a foundation for the church in Corinth (1 Cor. 3:10). Grace provided access to God for the Gentiles, and grace enabled Paul to take the message of grace to them (Eph. 3:7–8). The grace that calls one to and empowers one for ministry is inextricably bound to the experience of grace in redemption. Implicit in one's redemption is one's call to mission and ministry!

In verse 3 Paul speaks of the mystery which was once concealed but has now been revealed to him. Paul first used the word "mystery" in this letter in 1:9–10 to refer to God's comprehensive plan to establish a new creation under the headship of Christ. In the present context Paul focuses on one particular aspect of that greater mystery, and that is the inclusion of Gentiles as fellow members of the body of Christ (3:6). As we read this passage, we should not forget that Paul was a strict Pharisee and a persecutor of the early church. This reminder of Paul's past can help us understand why it required a revelation of a mystery to convince Paul to carry the gospel to the Gentiles.

At this point Paul refers to something he "wrote before in brief," which will provide greater understanding of his insight into the mystery of Christ "when you read" it. Many interpreters think this means something written earlier in the Ephesian letter and look to passages such as 1:9 or 2:19. That suggestion does not do justice to the indication that they will be able to read it at some time in the future. I think this is a reference to a letter which has already been written but has not yet been received by the present recipients of Ephesians. If the Colossian letter is also a circular letter which will be available to these readers in the near future, Paul may be referring to Colossians 1:24–29 and 4:3. In the Colossian letter Paul declares the truth that the indwelling Christ is the hope of glory for Jew and Gentile alike. In this passage he focuses on the truth that all in Christ are fellow members of the body.

Since a mystery requires revelation to be comprehended, it follows that "in other generations" (3:5) it was not made known to the sons of men. We should pause to ask, "What was not made clear?" The idea that God's blessings should be extended to the Gentiles, although often neglected by the Jews, was a constant theme of the Old Testament. In Romans 15:9–12, Paul quotes several Old Testament passages to authenticate his work among the Gentiles. What has now been made clear to the New Testament apostles and prophets is that the blessings that flowed from God through Israel would result in the creation of "one new man" by the incorporation of all people on the common ground of divine grace. The church made up of both Jews and

Gentiles is now seen clearly.

Notice the threefold emphasis made by compound words beginning with the word "fellow." Gentiles are now "fellow heirs," "fellow members," and "fellow partakers." It was God's eternal and unchanging plan that Jews and Gentiles be joint heirs "through the gospel." These previously unexpected blessings for the Gentiles are "in Christ" and thus now made known through the gospel. Paul's conversion led to a complete transformation of his thinking. He had once viewed Jesus as a dangerous heretic, but now he saw Him as the Christ, the Son of God. His view of the Gentiles was just as radically altered. They are fellow heirs, meaning they share fully in the heavenly riches of God. They are fellow members of the body, meaning they are now Paul's family. They are fellow partakers of the promise of life and salvation in Christ.

Has your thinking about your fellowman and his need to participate equally in the blessings available only through the gospel been radically altered by your conversion? What evidence can you give?

With absolute wonder and awe, Paul now considers his ministry in this new community of faith. "The gift of God's grace" (3:7) is a reference to his calling and empowering to be an apostle to the Gentiles. This calling was given "according to the working of His power" (3:7). This phrase is similar to that used in Ephesians 1:19 where Paul speaks of the resurrection power made available to the church and its members. To accomplish his ministry, Paul required both "the gift of God's grace" and "the working of His power." This was no abstract power but the energizing strength of the Holy Spirit working in and through Him. The same grace and power are available to us today.

The Manifold Wisdom of God . . . through the Church (3:8–11)

Paul's sense of amazement that God had chosen him continues to permeate this entire section. Paul considered himself to be "the very least of all saints" (3:8). This is neither feigned humility nor self-deprecation. Paul may be thinking of his shameful behavior as a persecutor of the church. The more Paul contemplated the greatness of God's grace, the more he recognized his own unworthiness. It was overwhelming to Paul that God would allow him to preach the "unfathomable riches of Christ" to the Gentiles. "Unfathomable" simply means that it is beyond man's comprehension. Notice that Paul's sense of unworthiness did not lead to inactivity but to passionate service to the One who had shown him grace.

It was Paul's privilege to "bring to light" (3:9) the mystery of this one new body made of Jew and Gentile which "for ages has been hidden in God." The church of the Lord Jesus Christ was no new creation based on Israel's failure to fully claim God's blessings. It was in no way an afterthought. An omniscient God has no afterthoughts. This mystery, now revealed, had been purposed and cherished by God from the beginning of time. The reference to God as Creator not only underlines God's power, but it also reminds us that before creation God chose His people in Christ (cf. 1:4)—Jew and Gentile alike—to be His community.

Paul now moves to a thought so profound it

should cause readers of every generation to catch their breath. He declares that the ministry of the church will reach beyond the constraints of this world order and time to show the manifold wisdom of God to rulers and authorities in the heavenly places. God's creation of one new man in Christ—His church—is an object lesson to the inhabitants of the heavenly places. The expression "the rulers and the authorities" used here and in Ephesians 6:12 probably includes both good and evil spiritual beings.

The word translated "manifold" can also be translated "variegated" and is used in classical Greek to describe the beauty of embroidered cloth. The church of the first century broke barriers that were considered impenetrable. Made up of Jew and Gentile, male and female, slave and free, this magnificent church, which would declare God's manifold wisdom for all eternity, was "in accordance with the eternal purpose which He carried out in Christ Jesus our Lord" (3:11). Jesus came to establish His church, which is tasked with completing His kingdom activity on earth.

Behind and beyond all the events of the world's history, God is working out His eternal purpose. He is not responding on the fly, but is working out a plan that was conceived in eternity past and is being accomplished daily. We who are "in Christ" and thus "in His body" are now caught up into His divine purpose, which spans eternity. When you read these verses, the passage where Jesus is first declared to be the Messiah by Peter should come to mind (Matt. 16:13–20). Once confessed as Messiah, Jesus declared His intention to build His church. To the church is given "the keys of the kingdom" and such authority that the very gates of hell cannot stand against it.

The emphasis on Christ's work through His church is emphasized by the fullness of His name—"Christ Jesus our Lord" (3:11). "Christ" speaks of His preexistent kingship, "Jesus" refers to His incarnate life, and "Lord" speaks of His position over the whole universe. "Christ Jesus our Lord" pours out His blessing on the church enabling it to express His fullness in the world (1:23) and declare His manifold wisdom to the rulers and authorities.

Boldness and Confident Access (3:12–13)

Before Paul returns to his prayer (3:14), he looks at one practical aspect of the eternal purpose of God accomplished in Christ. It gives believers "boldness and confident access through faith in Him" (3:12). Paul has already spoken of "our access in one Spirit to the Father" (2:18). Since the one through whom we have access is the same as the one in whom God's eternal purpose is accomplished, we can come into His presence with boldness and confidence.

"Boldness" is freedom of utterance or plainness of speech. The word translated "boldness" was used in classical Greek to signify the free speech, which was the right of every citizen of a democratic state. Members of His body, who are now also citizens of heaven, have ability and confidence to approach God directly with no intermediary apart from Christ. "Confidence" expresses a similar idea but is more personal in nature. Faith in Christ and the assurance of forgiveness of sin allows us to approach God with personal confidence.

Based on this newfound boldness and confidence, Paul returns to the matter of his present imprisonment. Knowing that Paul was imprisoned could cause his readers to lose heart. Paul wants them to be assured that his present circumstances are the direct consequences of His obedience to God's eternal plan to bring Jews and Gentiles together into one new man. Paul's sufferings are actually on their behalf, and thus they can find a reason for glorying in them.

How does it make you feel to be part of a community whose roots stretch back to eternity past and whose impact will be eternal?

FOR MEMORY AND MEDITATION

"So that the manifold wisdom of God might now be made known through the church to the rulers and authorities in the heavenly places." Ephesians 3:10

Beyond All We Ask
or Think

CHAPTER 6

Focal Text: Ephesians 3:14–21

What is your boldest prayer or greatest dream for your church? I can tell you without hesitation that it is far less than what God is prepared and able to do.

Paul once again takes up the prayer he started in 3:1 but interrupted by an excurses on his unexpected role in the unveiling of God's plan to display His manifold wisdom through the church. His prayer, now resumed, has added impact when one considers what he has just said about the role of the church in revealing God's multifaceted wisdom. When God brings dead men to life and unites them in one community, even the rulers in heavenly places are required to take notice.

I Bow My Knees (3:14–15)

This prayer is given greater intensity by the phrase, "I bow my knees before the Father." Normally Jews stood for prayer. Kneeling at prayer was an expression of deep emotion or earnestness. At great events such as the dedication of the temple, the martyrdom of Stephen, Peter at the deathbed of Dorcas, Paul bidding farewell on his journey to Jerusalem, and Jesus in the garden, we find people kneeling to pray. Since the church has been tasked and empowered to display God's manifold wisdom, Paul is compelled to bow humbly in prayer.

49

He addresses God as "the Father, from whom every family in heaven and on earth derives its name" (3:14b–15). God, as Father, is the only "underived" Father. The name "Father" did not go up from earth to the Creator but came down from heaven to man. Mortal man would never have been so bold as to address the sovereign Creator of everything as "Father" had not God given them that privilege. By virtue of creation, God is the rightful Father of every person and every people group on earth. Yet only in Christ are we privileged to address Him personally as "Abba, Father" (cf. Matt. 6:9). In Romans 8, Paul declared that those who are "sons of God" can cry out "Abba! Father!" (vv. 14–15). The Father desires that all who are His children by creation become His children by redemption. To make this possible is the task of the church, which is designed to display His manifold wisdom and commissioned to go into the entire world.

Strengthened with Power (3:16–17a)

The ministry and opportunity given to the church are clearly impossible in human strength, and thus the first request is for supernatural empowering. Here, as in 1:19, the apostle heaps synonyms for power one upon the other. The term translated "to be strengthened" means "to be made strong or capable." "Power" is from the Greek word *dunamis*, from which we get the English word dynamite. Literally, we are made capable by dynamite-like power in the core of our being.

In case you are thinking this promise of empowering does not apply to you, notice that it is not based on any human attainment or natural ability. Our empowering is "according to the riches of His glory" (3:16). The word glory is often used in the Bible to speak of God's manifest presence. In Old Testament days God's glory was frequently seen in dramatic events such as a flaming mountain or a burning bush. But these spectacular events in nature could not compare with God's glory made manifest in the person of Jesus. "And the Word became flesh, and dwelt among us, and we saw His glory, glory as of the only begotten from the Father, full of grace and truth" (John 1:14).

Think about it! Our empowering for ministry is based on the riches of God's glory. This means that God desires to indwell us with His Spirit in such a manner that His presence is made known through His church as clearly as it was in His Son.

The strength for ministry comes from the personal indwelling of the Holy Spirit. The same Spirit who indwelt and empowered Jesus' ministry now indwells us. He takes up His abode "in the inner man" (3:16). In 2 Corinthians 4:16, Paul contrasts the inner man with the outer man. The outer man is decaying. Simply put, our earthly body is impacted by the ravages of age. Nonetheless, our inner man is being renewed daily. The inner man is the true you; it is the core of your being, the deep seat of your personality. For the believer the inner man delights in the law of God (Rom. 7:22). The Holy Spirit dwells in the inner man, transforming us into the image of God and empowering us for effective kingdom ministry.

Know the Unknowable Love of Christ (3:17–19a)

We are strengthened with power "so that Christ may dwell" (3:17) in our hearts. The tense of the verb translated "dwell" is aorist, indicating that Christ is taking up His abode in our hearts. Although the verbal expression is different, there is a striking parallel with the promise Jesus gave His disciples as He was preparing them for His departure. "If anyone loves Me, he will keep My word; and My Father will love him, and We will come to him and make Our abode with him" (John 14:23). The empowering of the Spirit and the indwelling of Christ are not two different experiences but are knit together by the triune God. "Faith" is the necessary response that opens one's heart to the permanent and full indwelling of Christ (cf. Rev. 3:20).

When one is fully indwelt by Christ, it will be evidenced not only by supernatural power but also by incomprehensible love. Paul employs both architectural and biological images to discuss the importance of love to the spiritual life. If you glance back at Ephesians 2:19–22, you will notice that Paul uses similar images to speak of the church which is God's one new man. These two passages are intentionally linked to one another. Growing faith is not simply dependent on ever-increasing intellectual and theoretical knowledge about God. True personal knowledge of God is unattainable without love which is experienced in relationship with others. The study of doctrine which does not issue in loving relationships leads to a sterile pharisaic religion.

Paul describes love in four dimensions—breadth, length, height, and depth. Three-dimensional movies have recently become quite the rage. Their success has led to the introduction of 3–D televisions. This is not a new phenomenon. I can remember, as a young pre-teen, putting on cardboard glasses with one green lens and one red lens that enabled me to see certain comic books and movies in 3–D. But Paul prays that we will know a love so vast it can only be described using four dimensions. However, we are not simply to give literal meanings to these words. Rather, we are to feel and experience with our mind, heart, and intuition the many dimensions of love and allow Christ to weave them into the fabric of our lives so that it expresses itself in our everyday relationships.

Perhaps you noticed that the words of this prayer seem to request what is clearly impossible. How can we know something "which surpasses knowledge"? In Romans 5:7–8, Paul indicates that we can conceive of a man giving his life for a good man, but God's love was such that Christ died for ungodly sinners. We cannot comprehend such self-giving and undeserved love. It is simply too much for our language to express or our mind to fathom.

The key to understanding this apparent paradox is found in the context. Underline the four little words—"with all the saints" (3:18). None of us have the breadth or depth of experience to comprehend fully the love of Christ, but all of us together can progressively comprehend the incomprehensible. When we gather as His church, each of us brings our own personal experience of Christ's love to that encounter. I may have experienced His love in the midst of tragedy or grief, while you may have experienced His love through events of great happiness. As we share our personal knowledge of Christ's love, each of us gains a broader picture of the seemingly unknowable love of Christ. It is vain for any individual to think that he/she can attain spiritual maturity and strength isolated from fellow believers. When we accept Christ as Savior, we are baptized into the community of believers by the Holy Spirit (1 Cor. 12:13).

Filled Up to All the Fullness of God (3:19b)

The term "fullness" is a key word used frequently in the Colossian and Ephesian letters. In Colossians, where Paul was battling heresy that questioned the uniqueness of Christ, he declares, "For it was the Father's good pleasure for all the fullness to dwell in Him" (Col. 1:19). In other words, Jesus—who is the image of the invisible God (Col. 1:15), the One through whom creation was accomplished (Col. 1:16), and the Head of the church (Col. 1:17)—reveals God completely. We call to mind the words Jesus used to encourage His disciples when He told them of His coming crucifixion. "He who has seen Me has seen the Father" (John 14:9).

In the Ephesian letter Paul dares to apply the word "fullness" to the church. In his first prayer, recorded in 1:18–23, Paul prays that his readers will know the hope of His calling, the riches of the glory of His inheritance in the saints, and the surpassing greatness of His power toward those who believe. He then describes this power by looking at the resurrection and coronation of Christ, which was accomplished for the church, "which is His body, the fullness of Him who fills all in all" (1:23). The church is designed, commissioned, and empowered to express God's fullness on earth today as Christ did during His incarnation. Does that idea stagger you? Does your church express God's fullness in your community in the same manner Christ did during His incarnation?

In our present text, Paul prays that his readers will "be filled up to all the fullness of God." The preposition "to" or "unto" suggests a progressive filling up to the mark of fullness. In Christ the fullness is already ours as an inheritance, but it must increasingly be realized in the daily life of the church. Paul will explain how this happens in his discussion of the gifted community. Simply stated, the "fullness" is appropriated as every gifted member finds his/her place in the body and fully uses his/her gifts for the building up of the body (4:11–16). Gifted service in and through the church must be the goal and passion of every believer until the church comes down out of heaven as the bride of Christ.

Beyond All That We Ask or Think (3:20–21)

Paul concludes his prayer with a spontaneous outburst of praise. While the prayer is bold beyond comprehension, Paul triumphantly praises God who is able to do "far more abundantly beyond all that we ask or think" (3:20). No matter how far the thought or desire of man can reach, God can do infinitely more. Paul coins a "super superlative" to express the exceeding abundance of God's power available to the church. There is simply no limit to His power. The only limitations are our words to describe it and our faith to embrace it.

This is not theoretical power we sing about in

worship or discuss in our small groups; it is actual power "that works within us." Don't miss the truth that God has chosen to act with power on earth by using the human instrumentation of those willing to follow and obey Him. It is not enough to pray that God will reveal His mighty hand on earth or in our community; we must make ourselves available.

You may be wondering why God chooses to work through a seemingly insignificant group of people like the church—your church? Because He desires to receive glory through the church and in Christ Jesus (3:21)! In and through the church, the body of Christ and the bride of Christ, God is glorified. When we speak of God being glorified, we most often think of Christ enthroned on the right hand of the Father where His people are raised up with Him. Yet we must not miss the truth that here on earth, where we still inhabit these human bodies, God is glorified as His people work together in gifted community to express His fullness.

The church is the place of the outworking of God's kingdom activity on earth, and even in heaven it has the task of declaring His manifold wisdom (3:10). Yet the church never takes glory to itself but always reflects it on Christ. Now, in this age, Christ and His church—the bride and the Bridegroom—are seen together giving to God unceasing glory until the end of the age. How can you assist your church in this role? Do you know your place in the gifted ministry of your church?

FOR MEMORY AND MEDITATION

"Now to Him who is able to do far more abundantly beyond all that we ask or think, according to the power that works within us, to Him be the glory in the church and in Christ Jesus to all generations forever and ever. Amen." Ephesians 3:20–21

The Gifted Community Expressing God's Fullness

CHAPTER 7

Focal Text: Ephesians 4:1–16

If you have ever witnessed rowing at the university or Olympic level, you have a great picture of how the gifted church should function. When everyone gets their oars in the water at the same moment, takes the same length stroke, and then cleanly removes their oars, the boat seems to glide effortless on the surface of the water. When each gifted member fully uses his/her gift(s) for the good of the body, the church advances God's kingdom activity.

The Worthy Walk (4:1–3)

The small connector "therefore" has big implications. In light of the many blessings believers have received and the high calling of the church, it is imperative that all members of the body "walk" in a manner worthy of their calling. Believers must never forget that we were once "sons of disobedience" (2:2), who deserved God's wrath; but God who is "rich in mercy" (2:4) made us alive with Christ and brought us into His own household (2:19–22). It is incumbent for us to live in a manner that speaks of the high cost of our redemption and calling. The reception of the gospel comes with the obligation to live in a manner that suits Christ's name because we are His (cf. Phil. 1:29).

The first three chapters of Ephesians are predominately doctrinal in nature, but in the remainder of the letter Paul will turn his attention to the practical application of that doctrine. Doctrine is never a matter of mere contemplation; it is transformational truth that drives Christian conduct. Character and conduct must correspond to one's creed.

Throughout our study of Ephesians, we have noticed the importance of "community" for our own personal development. This passage is no different! The description of the worthy walk begins with the phrase "showing tolerance for one another in love." Love enables us to overcome the difficulties inherent in human relationships. These first few verses are not about being virtuous but about living in harmony with God's call. We can compare the attributes necessary for the worthy walk in community with the fruit of the Spirit.

Humility and gentleness are inextricably bound together. Humility is a distinctly biblical virtue, which was actually considered a vice in the Greek world. Humility is not a pious personal put-down. Such false expressions of humility are often little more than inverted conceit that begs for human affirmation. True humility comes from a biblical assessment of who we are in Christ. Proper evaluation of oneself rules out both arrogant display and cowering self-pity.

Humility, gentleness, and patience are the divine attributes that enable believers to accept one another in love and thus preserve the unity of the Spirit (4:3). The various terms Paul employs in verse 2 somewhat overlap in meaning. Taken together they are intended to combat arrogance, harshness, and intolerance in personal relationships. These practical expressions of love are the necessary foundation for the proper functioning of the gifted community.

Notice that believers are challenged to be "diligent to preserve the unity of the Spirit" (4:3). Unity is both a gift of God mediated by the Spirit and a goal toward which we must strive. While we cannot create unity, we can and must make every effort to preserve it. Unity is to be pursued through the edifying use of one's gift(s) (4:13). The phrase "in the bond of peace" (4:3) reminds us that peace will be the result of a unified community. Since God is the author of peace, sowing discord among the brethren is a detriment to effective ministry and an affront to God.

Unity, the Foundation for Gifted Ministry (4:4–6)

Living together in community is challenging when one considers the variety of temperaments and differences in preferences that come from our diverse social, racial, generational, and economic backgrounds. To combat the forces that could lead to disunity, Paul articulates a sevenfold expression of unity that is one of the most eloquent compositions in all of Scripture. Some commentators believe Paul may have been quoting a fragment from an early Christian hymn.

The first triad—"one body," "one Spirit," "one hope of your calling"—reminds us of several great truths developed in the earlier chapters of this letter. "One body" refers to the church as the body of Christ. "One Spirit" speaks of the Holy Spirit who gives each individual access to the Father and thus brings diverse members together for a dwelling of God (2:18–22). The church is a living organism, made up of persons who have in common the shared experience of the Spirit. Thus it derives its life, unity, empowering, and gifts for ministry from the Spirit. "One hope of your calling" means the hope which is received by virtue of one's response to the call to salvation and mission (1:18).

The second triad—"one Lord," "one faith," and "one baptism"—reminds the readers of the moment when they publicly confessed Jesus as Lord. "One Lord" is not merely an expression of shared belief; it is a common allegiance to one transcendent Lord. Neither cliquishness, nor personal ambition, nor disputes about nonessentials can be allowed to compromise unity. The common relationship to Christ expressed visibly through baptism has broken down every barrier. In the Corinthian letter Paul wrote: "For by one Spirit we were all baptized into one body" (1 Cor. 12:13).

Paul concludes with a reference to God whose essential "oneness" is the basis for the unity of all His people. This statement clearly reflects the Old Testament declaration that the God of Israel is the one true God. The phrase "who is over all and through all and in all" indicates that everything is God created, God sustained, and God filled. God Himself is the source of our unity, and anything that creates disunity disrupts and diminishes the work of the church, which was designed to express the fullness of God.

The Triumphant King Gifts His Church (4:7–10)

Unity does not mean uniformity. Thus Paul turns now to discuss the endless variety of gifts that God distributes to make us dependent on Him and interdependent in fellowship. In His discussion of spiritual gifts in 1 Corinthians 12, Paul speaks of the Spirit as the distributer of the gifts. In the Roman letter (12:3), God is the one who allots gifts to each believer. In this letter Paul has focused throughout on the exalted and triumphant Christ pouring out blessings on His church, and thus he understandably declares, "But to each one of us grace was given according to the measure of Christ's gift" (4:7). Contemplating that all three persons of the Trinity cooperate in the distribution of the gifts and the equipping of the body is an overwhelming thought.

Don't read this passage so quickly that you miss the phrase "to each one of us." No member of the body is ungifted or unimportant to the mission of the church. In this passage Paul uses the simple word "grace" *(charis)* rather than the more complex word "manifestation of grace" *(charismata)* which he used in 1 Corinthians. Paul has already used "grace" to discuss his apostolic gifting and calling (3:2, 7–8). The context makes clear that "grace" here means an individualized expression of grace which enables us to accomplish a unique and God-given ministry for the Head of the church.

How does the exalted Christ express His fullness in the world through His church? He gives gifts to men and women and, in turn, gives those gifted persons to His church. To affirm the triumphant King's role in gifting His church, Paul quotes Psalm 68:18. When you read Psalm 68, you will notice an important alteration that emphasizes the giving of gifts to men rather than receiving gifts from men. It is possible that the Spirit inspired Paul to paraphrase the psalm, adapting it to suit his purpose. It is, however, interesting that the Targum on the psalm (an Aramaic translation or paraphrase of some parts of the Old Testament) contains the same alteration. Appropriately enough, Psalm 68 was associated with Pentecost in synagogue worship. The point of the quotation is clear: the victorious King is leading in a triumphal procession and bestowing gifts on those who line the parade route.

The themes of the exaltation of Christ, His dominion over all powers, and His filling of all things through the church are emphasized throughout Colossians and Ephesians. By applying this Psalm to Christ, Paul underlines the total sufficiency of the exalted Lord to equip the church to complete His kingdom work. This truth strikes a telling blow against any heresy that would devalue Christ or diminish His church. Your community and the world desperately need to see the fullness of God displayed in and through your church.

In Ephesians 4:9–10 Paul comments on the term "ascended" to fortify the affirmation that the resurrected Lord is the Giver of the gifts. Christ, who previously descended from heaven, has now ascended triumphant over all powers, including death and the grave. His ministry now is to "fill all things," and He accomplishes this work by placing gifted men and women in His church. This singular truth should shake us from the lethargy of playing church and create an insatiable desire to know and use our gifts for His glory.

Gifted Leaders Equipping Gifted Members (4:11–12)

The brief gift list in this section is unique, focusing only on leadership gifts. Nonetheless, all members are clearly gifted for ministry since the leaders are to equip "the saints for the work of service" (4:12). The apostles and prophets refer to New Testament apostles and prophets who had a foundational role in the establishment of the church (cf. Eph. 2:20; 3:5). The second pair, evangelists and teaching pastors are required in every generation. "Evangelists" may refer to the church-planting missionaries of the first century. The pastor/teacher is sometimes referred to as an "elder" or a "bishop" in other contexts. The New Testament church was more focused on function than title.

Verse 12 focuses on the pastor/teacher's role in the local church. The word translated "equipping" only occurs here in the New Testament. The idea is to enable "saints" to discover their gifted role in the body and then to bring them to a level of spiritual fitness that enables them to serve effectively in their ministry role. In case you struggle with the word "saint" and think you don't qualify, it means that you have been separated unto God for service. You do qualify by virtue of your redemption. The equipping of the saints has the singular goal of "building up the body of Christ" so that it may accomplish its global mission.

The Results of Gifted Ministry (4:13–16)

Unity, which is a gift of the Spirit (4:3), becomes reality as the gifted leaders and members use their gifts to build up the body. The word "attain" is used in Acts for travelers arriving at their destination. The phrase "unity of the faith" and "knowledge of the Son of God" are bound together both by the Greek construction and by the context of the sentence. "Unity of the faith" is not simply the acceptance of a collection of dogmas; it is much more personal. It is unity in our "knowledge

65

of the Son of God." It is an increasing, personal acquaintance with Christ that allows us to attain the unity given by the Spirit.

As we grow in unity and knowledge, maturity, which is measured by the "stature which belongs to the fullness of Christ" (4:13), is achieved. The ultimate goal of our gifted ministry and resulting maturity is that we might express the fullness of Christ. The church is already the "fullness" by virtue of the resurrection (1:23), and now the church is challenged to attain to that "fullness" through the spiritual growth and gifted ministry of its members.

This growing maturity will ultimately result in doctrinal stability. The immature run after every wind of doctrine and are easily taken in by the trickery of men. "Tossed here and there" indicates the action of turbulent waves on a small boat. Paul uses another word that speaks of fraud in games of dice. He employs several different images to show the danger of false teaching to the immature and unconnected Christian.

In contrast to the dizzying turbulence experienced by the immature, Paul concludes with a picture of healthy and balanced growth. "Speaking the truth in love" indicates a life where doctrine and behavior line up. What is upheld as nonnegotiable truth and the manner in which it is upheld must be the same. The context of truthful, loving community enables believers to "grow up in all aspects into Him who is the head, even Christ" (4:15).

From Christ alone the body derives its whole capacity for growth and activity. The phrase translated "being fitted" occurs only here and at Ephesians 2:21.

It pictures the intimate relationship of each member to the other. While the body depends on Christ for its growth and work, His provision for the whole is based on the proper working and interrelationship of each part. You are an essential "joint" through which Christ accomplishes His kingdom work on earth.

FOR MEMORY AND MEDITATION

"But to each one of us grace was given according to the measure of Christ's gift." (Ephesians 4:7)

Off with the Old,
On with the New

Focal Text: Ephesians 4:17–32

We are familiar with the famous New Year's declaration, "Out with the old, in with the new." After discussing the importance of the gifted community, Paul turns his attention to the lifestyle of followers of Christ. He uses several different images to picture the radical contrast between the behavior of the saved and the unsaved. Once again he employs the image of walking to speak of the conduct of one's life, but he now adds the imagery of changing garments: off with the old, on with the new!

While the first half of this section focuses on personal transformation, the second half moves quickly to the impact of one's personal behavior on the corporate community. Christianity knows neither rampant individualism nor determined isolationism. We are born again into a Christian family—the body of Christ—and our personal behavior affects the entire community.

No Longer Walk in Futility (4:17–19)

Before one can begin an effective new way of life, he/she must completely abandon the old way of life. Paul gives this statement added emphasis and apostolic authority by indicating that he is affirming it "together with the Lord." Many of his readers were former Gentiles (pagans); others were Jews, who shared in the sin nature. But now they are no longer Jew or Gentile;

they are a new race of people who transcend all other categories—followers of Christ.

The cautionary "walk no longer" indicates that while the old way has been renounced, believers still live in a fallen world surrounded by people who continually walk in the futility of their mind. As you read verses 17–19, underline the devastating and dark terms and phrases that describe life before Christ. "Futility"! "Darkened in . . . understanding"! "Excluded from the life of God"! "Ignorance"! "Hardness of . . . heart"! "Callous"! "Sensuality"! "Impurity"! "Greediness"!

People without Christ conduct their daily life in the "futility of their mind" (v. 17). This means that no matter how successful or prosperous people might appear, if they live without regard for their Creator, they are living in futility. Without personal knowledge of God, all is vanity; man has no sense of his ultimate purpose and thus no transcendent goal. When an individual or a society loses the concept of a holy God who is Creator and Sustainer, they lose the true object and perfection of human life. This is why the psalmist declares; "The fool has said in his heart, 'There is no God'" (Ps. 14:1a).

Man who ignores God is darkened in his understanding because he discounts God who is the source of all truth. While man may accumulate knowledge, without God in the equation, he has no true wisdom because he begins from a false premise. The result is a downward spiral. Rejection of the truth of God excludes man from the life of God, which is life itself. Men are excluded from the life of God because of spiritual ignorance, which, in turn, leads to hardness of heart and insensitivity to spiritual truth. Man's spiritual death is the direct result of his ignorant refusal to have God in his life (cf. Rom. 1:28–32).

When men are past feeling ("having become callous"), they give themselves over to sensuality. It is possible for man to so deaden his conscience that he feels no conviction for sin. When this occurs, immoral behavior normally follows. "Every kind of impurity with greediness" speaks of sensuality in great measure. Impurity becomes the pursuit of one's life. In Romans 1:24–28, a passage with a similar emphasis, Paul tells us that one of the aspects of God's wrath is to give sinners up to their own choices with the terrible accompanying consequences.

Lay Aside and Put On (4:20–24)

"But you" provides a strong contrast. Believers can no longer walk in futility because they "did not learn Christ in this way" (v. 20). Christ is so much the embodiment of His teaching that His teaching cannot be fully comprehended without coming to know Him. Further, to know Christ is to accept and obey His teaching. Verse 21 does not suggest that Paul is casting doubt on their conversion experience. He is simply calling upon his readers to verify their confession of faith through behavior. We could summarize thus: "If you know anything about Christ at all, you know that He lived and commanded a lifestyle that is vastly different from that practiced by pagans." Paul concludes with the affirmation that "truth is in Jesus" (4:21). Man has no excuse for living in the futility of his mind since the truth about God was made manifest through the incarnation, in the life and words of Jesus.

Paul gives them a simple three-step formula for their new life in Christ—put off, "be renewed," "put on." The first step in transformational living is to "put off." The imagery of "putting off" and "putting on" is found frequently in New Testament writings (Rom. 13:12; Col. 3:9; Heb. 12:1; Jas. 1:21; 1 Pet. 2:1). This imagery may have been part of an early church "new members' class," teaching new believers how to live. To put off the "old self" means to abandon all that belongs to the old way of life. The Greek tense here indicates a decisive act of putting off, a volitional turning from an "old," futile way of life.

Second, the believer must "be renewed in the spirit of your mind" (v. 23). The present-tense verb is used to indicate the need for continual renewal. The mind is the center of one's thinking and processing of truth. The mind can be used to process spiritual truth, or it can be used to focus on merely natural matters. In Romans 12:2, Paul tells us that man can either be conformed to the world or be "transformed by the renewing of the mind." In Colossians, the companion letter to Ephesians, Paul instructs his readers, "Set your mind on the things above, not on the things that are on earth" (3:2). The renewal of the mind occurs as we read and meditate on the Word of God, allowing it to shape our thought and behavior.

Having put off the old man (the nature of Adam), they must now put on the new man (Christ) whose very nature is given to believers through the process of new birth. In Colossians 3:10 Paul describes believers as persons who have "put on the new self who is being renewed to a true knowledge according to the image of the One who created him."

Believers require constant renewal of the mind in order to progressively and comprehensively put on the new man. The image of God in man was marred by sin, and life in full fellowship with God was lost. Now through Christ man can be recreated, restored to the image of God, and experience intimacy with God.

God is righteous and holy, qualities that were perfectly manifest in Christ. It follows that the individual who "puts on" Christ will be characterized by these same qualities. What occurs through the putting off, the continual renewal, and the putting on is the creation of Christlikeness in the believer.

Members of One Another (4:25–32)

Once again Paul employs the linking word "therefore," which signifies that he is now going to list the implications of what it means for one to put on the new man. Does it surprise you that Paul immediately moves to discuss the believer's life in community? While salvation is and must be an individual and personal experience, it will always have a corporate dynamic.

Once again Paul employs the "laying aside" imagery that he used in verse 22 above. "Falsehood" is a characteristic of the old man and the sin nature, and thus it must be discarded. However, it is not enough merely to discard sinful behavior; one must replace it with righteous behavior. In this case falsehood is replaced with truth. The phrase "speak truth each one of you with his neighbor" is a quotation from Zechariah 8:16 with an important modification. The "to" in Zechariah is now "with," emphasizing the integral connection of one member to another—"for we are members of one another" (v. 25). Since God is truth, any deceit is an offense against Him and a hindrance to the proper functioning of His body. In Ephesians 4:15 Paul writes that the body grows up in every respect as members speak the truth in love.

Paul moves next to anger, which negatively impacts the fellowship of the church. This saying is from Psalm 4:4. Anger itself, particularly if it is righteous anger as exemplified by Jesus, is not sin. But anger can cause man to sin. Often so-called "righteous indignation" is little more than wounded pride. One way to keep anger in check so that it does not lead to sin is by limiting its duration—"Do not let the sun go down on your anger" (4:26). Paul may still be thinking about Psalm 4:4, which concludes: "Meditate in your heart upon your bed, and be still." When I submit my anger to the Lord, I will attempt to resolve the issue that caused my angry response. Even when I can't resolve the issue, I can be reconciled in my heart by forgiving the person who offended me and by choosing not to become bitter.

A positive response to anger is critical to my spiritual well-being and to the health of the church. If I nurse hurt feelings and become bitter, I provide the devil an opportunity to exploit my anger for his purposes. He can cause me to have unkind thoughts toward a fellow member. He can turn my anger into a grudge, which hinders the fellowship and function of the body.

The converted thief must not only give up stealing; he must do good work with his own hands so that he will have an excess to share with those in need.

The Christian welcomes hard work since it is the duty of every authentic believer (cf. 1 Thess. 4:11; 2 Thess. 3:1–12). Even our Christian work ethic is connected to our life in community! For the Christian, giving provides the motivation for getting. Since the ethic of labor is placed in the context of its impact on the body of Christ, we must also think of members of the body who "steal" by failing to give time, effort, or resources for the work of the body.

The "unwholesome word" is to be replaced by a word which "is good for edification" (4:29). The term "unwholesome" has the connotation of rotten and thus worthless. The believer replaces foul and worthless language with a word that meets the need of the moment and thus gives "grace to those who hear." Because we are now indwelt by the Holy Spirit, we can speak words that are both timely and life giving. Solomon wrote: "A man has joy in an apt answer, and how delightful is a timely word!" (Prov. 15:23). In Colossians 4:6, Paul speaks of speech which, like salt, adds flavor to life of the hearer. My dad taught me to ask three questions before I spoke: "Is it true? Is it necessary? Is it helpful?" We need to ask ourselves, "Do my words hurt or heal?"

Paul's instructions about dealing with anger were followed with a warning about giving opportunity to the devil. The teaching about one's language is followed by a warning about grieving the Holy Spirit (v. 30). Sins of the tongue are wrongs done to and felt by the Holy Spirit who indwells both the speaker and the listener. These sins frequently destroy the unity of the body which is given by the Spirit (Eph. 4:3). This warning is given gravity by the full reference, "Holy

Spirit of God" (v. 30). We have been sealed in the Spirit, waiting the day of the Lord's return (cf. Eph. 1:14), and thus our speech must reflect His presence in our lives.

Verses 31–32 serve as somewhat of a summary statement. To avoid grieving the Spirit, we must set aside every attitude, response, and behavior which threatens the unity of the church. Bitterness is an attitude that refuses reconciliation and thus poisons one's life. Wrath and anger are often listed together (Rom. 2:8; Col. 3:8). They are the quick outbursts of anger caused by personal provocation. "Clamor" describes the angry person who desires that everyone hear his grievance. "Slander" translates the Greek word which means "blasphemy," a word often used in terms of speaking against God. When we slander our fellow believer, who bears the image of Christ, we blaspheme. "Malice" is bad feelings of any and every kind. Paul calls for total abstinence from every thought and emotion that would lead us to speak against or do evil to another.

Paul ends with positive behavior patterns that must replace the destructive ones just mentioned. Kindness is love made practical. The call to forgive one another as we have been forgiven may be an echo of the Lord's Prayer. We must forgive freely and completely even when it appears to us that forgiveness is undeserved. After all, isn't that how God forgave us?

FOR MEMORY AND MEDITATION

"And put on the new self, which in the likeness of God has been created in righteousness and holiness of the truth." Ephesians 4:24

Follow the Leader

CHAPTER 9

Focal Text: Ephesians 5:1–21

One of my favorite childhood games was Follow the Leader. The rules were simple. A leader was chosen who began the game by doing some stunt he believed his followers could not duplicate. It was usually a harmless game until the leader attempted a foolish trick that caused a follower to be injured. That was the end of the game.

Have you ever considered that each day we participate in a real-life version of Follow the Leader? The leader we follow will impact every area of our life. Paul begins chapter 5 with the challenge: "Therefore be imitators of God, as beloved children." He speaks of four areas of conduct in which we must imitate or "walk" after God—love, purity, light, and wisdom.

Walk in Love (5:1–2)

We are called to be imitators of God, based on our relationship to Him as children to the Father. This is the only place in the New Testament that believers are instructed to imitate God. We cannot ignore the immediate connection to the last verse of chapter 4 where Paul challenges us to forgive one another just as God in Christ has forgiven us. When Jesus taught His disciples to pray, He indicated that we should pray not only for forgiveness but also for the ability to forgive our debtors in the same measure and manner that we have been forgiven (Matt. 6:12).

In the Sermon on the Mount, Jesus challenged

77

believers to be perfect as their Father is perfect (Matt. 5:48). In that instance the call to be like one's heavenly Father is in the context of loving our enemies and praying for those who persecute us. Both the challenge to forgive others as God has forgiven us and the challenge to love one's enemies are beyond our ability in the real-life game of Follow the Leader. That is precisely why this section In Ephesians ends with the command to be filled with the Spirit. Only the Holy Spirit can enable us to imitate God as we walk in love.

In verse 2, with the challenge to "walk in love, just as Christ also loved you," Paul expands the matter of imitating God to every area of one's life. The word "walk" means "the conduct of one's life." The imagery of walking indicates that love is not a one-time emotional response to God but the ongoing pattern of the Christian's daily life. The love we are to imitate is the self-giving love that prompted Christ to give Himself up for us, "an offering and a sacrifice to God as a fragrant aroma" (v. 2). The language is that of the Levitical law of sacrifice. When our lives are a self-giving sacrifice to the Father, we can forgive our fellowman and thus fill heaven with a sweet fragrance (cf. 2 Cor. 2:14–16).

Following our Leader is no game! It calls for us to live in a sacrificial manner that spreads forgiveness and returns good to those who do evil to us.

Walk in Purity (5:3–5)

Catalogs of vices were common in writings of both pagan moralists and in Jewish polemic against the excesses of paganism. In Paul's writings the catalogs of vices are given a uniquely Christian context by the indication that those who practice such pagan behaviors have no inheritance in the kingdom of Christ or God.

The twenty-first century and the first century have much in common. Sexual immorality and other forms of sexually impurity were commonplace among pagans, and thus converts to Christianity had to be warned that such behavior is not proper among the "saints," those who have separated themselves unto Christ.

The word translated "immorality" is from the Greek word *porneia,* from which we get the word pornography. It covers sexual perversion of any and every kind. Do you think it is odd that Paul would move from a call to self-giving love to the issue of sexual perversion? Adultery, and all other sexual sin, is true love's greatest perversion, and thus it is given particular attention because it distorts man's understanding of authentic love available in and through Christ.

You may have been surprised to see "greed" listed along with immorality and impurity, but Paul is moving from the outward manifestation of sin to the inner craving of one's heart. Sexual sin is a form of ruthless greed because it is selfish indulgence at the expense of others. No sexual sin is harmless because on every occasion someone is being exploited by the selfish gratification of another. Since believers are called to be holy as their Father is holy, immorality and impurity are not fitting for behavior, thought, or word. This includes crude sexual jokes or gossip about others' sexual sins.

In verse 4, Paul continues to enumerate conduct and conversation which are inappropriate for believers. "Filthiness" means "anything that would make a morally sensitive person ashamed or embarrassed." "Silly talk" indicates words without sense or profit. "Coarse jesting" speaks of humor which flirts with the borderline of impropriety. Paul does not prudishly forbid conversation about sexual matters, nor does he forbid healthy humor, but he does prohibit talk that demeans sexuality and harms the spiritual life. When one speaks of sex, possessions, or people, it should always be in a manner that acknowledges them as gifts of God, and thus it should be filled with "giving of thanks." Thanksgiving is filled with praise and as such is pure and uplifting.

Paul concludes this section on impurity with a solemn warning. These sins, along with all other unrepented sin, exclude men from God's kingdom. Only the regenerate can enter the kingdom. The habitual practice of sin bears witness to an unregenerate heart (cf. 1 Cor. 6:9–11).

Were you surprised that Paul included covetousness along with this listing of sexual sins? Further, he indicates that the covetous man is an idolater. Sexual sin is, at its heart, covetousness since it desires that which does not rightfully belong to one. It is idolatry because it causes man to set his affection on earthly things and thus puts an object of desire in the central place of one's heart, which God alone should occupy.

Walk as Children of Light (5:6–14)

There were persons in the first century who argued that sins of the flesh were irrelevant to one's spiritual life because they had to do with one's body and not one's soul. In Romans 6:1, Paul confronted those who argued that freedom from the law implied the freedom to sin. Such arguments, however they are stated or justified, are "empty words" (Eph. 5:6). All unrighteous behavior stands under the wrath of God.

In Ephesians 3:6, Paul declared that Jews and Gentiles were now "fellow heirs," "fellow members," and "fellow partakers" with Jews in the one body of Christ. To express these wonderful truths, he used compound words formed by adding the Greek prefix *syn* to each word. In this verse he uses another such compound to warn against being "partakers with them," meaning "the sons of disobedience." Those who have been joined to the body of Christ cannot be joined to the sons of disobedience.

To further illustrate the incompatibility of old patterns of pagan life with the new life found in Christ, Paul uses the images of light and darkness. When we declare that "God is Light" (1 John 1:5), we are speaking of His majesty, His glory, and His perfect holiness. John repeatedly tells us that Jesus is the light of the world (John 1:9; 8:12; 9:5). The opposite of light is darkness, which represents the world estranged from God. Those who have new life in Christ have been transferred from the realm of darkness to the realm of light (cf. 2 Cor. 4:6; Col. 1:13). Not only do the unredeemed live in darkness, but darkness is also in them—"You were formerly darkness" (Eph. 5:8). "But now you are Light in the Lord" (v. 8). This declaration reminds us of the Sermon on the Mount when Jesus declared that His followers were salt and light.

Paul commands his readers to behave according to their new nature—"walk as children of Light" (v. 8). Paul describes walking in the Light as bearing the fruit of Light. The fruit of Light, like the fruit of the Spirit, is not a matter of effort but one of surrender that allows the Light within to reveal itself in human flesh. Goodness, righteousness, and truth are produced by the true Light, which indwells us (v. 9).

The verb translated "trying to learn" in verse 10 is the same verb used by Paul in Romans 12:2 to speak of the believer's transformed behavior. In both places it means to know and do the will of God. We prove the will of God by putting it into practice. The Light of God is given to man, but it does not free men from the necessity of choosing to display that Light. Thus children of Light choose to please the Lord and not gratify their own selfish desires.

"Deeds of darkness" are "unfruitful" in comparison with the life that is the "fruit of the Light." Not only does the believer avoid participation in the unfruitful deeds of darkness, but he/she must expose them. The Christian's life should expose sin by its very brilliance. When we turn on a light in our house, it exposes filth that was hidden by darkness. The visible witness of the Light of our holy life allows us to avoid the disgrace of speaking of the sinful things that are done by the lost in darkness (5:12). This verse does not mean we can never speak out concerning moral depravity. For example, Paul spoke strongly about sexual sin in Romans 1:24–32. In this context Paul is appealing for a lifestyle that is such a contrast to darkness that it both exposes and reproves the life of darkness.

When light is present, "all things become visible" (5:13). When the Light of Christ shines from the life of His followers, it brings sinful man into a moment of crisis (cf. John 3:19–21). Our goal is that all those around us receive and become light. Paul concludes this section with a quotation whose essence is scriptural but which does not conform to any precise

Old Testament text. It may be a fragment of an early baptismal hymn. Appropriately, it uses three metaphors for turning to God—awakening from sleep, rising from the dead, and moving from darkness to light (5:14).

Walk in Wisdom (5:15–21)

Earlier in this letter Paul prayed that God would give his readers a "spirit of wisdom" (Eph. 1:17). Further, he indicated that God makes His "manifold wisdom" known through the church (Eph. 3:10). Those who are wise will be good stewards of time "because the days are evil" (5:16). The word for "time" is *kairos,* which speaks of a critical epoch or opportunity. Christians must see every day and every occasion as an opportunity to turn others from darkness to light. In the parallel passage in Colossians 4:5, Paul specifically links the use of one's time with the opportunity to witness to unbelieving neighbors. Failure to seize every opportunity to do God's will and work is foolish behavior (5:17).

The quotation against drunkenness is from the Septuagint (a Greek translation of the OT) translation of Proverbs 23:20. Drunkenness makes it impossible for one to seize each moment as an opportunity for doing the will of God. Paul quickly moves from the prohibition to a positive command—"be filled with the Spirit" (v. 18). Christian ethic does not take pleasure from our lives but replaces earthly pleasure with a higher and better pleasure. The Christian knows a better way than alcohol for living above the depression and monotony of life. The Greek tense of the verb is a present imperative, indicating that being filled with the Spirit is not a once-in-a-lifetime experience but rather an ongoing, life-changing process.

Verses 19–21 describe, in part, what the Spirit-filled life will look like. Rather than drunkenness, the exhilaration of the Spirit will be expressed in song and praise. The early disciples were accused of drunkenness when the Spirit filled them on the Day of Pentecost (Acts 2:13). Being filled with the Holy Spirit will be evidenced by a marked change in one's behavior!

"Speaking to one another" reminds us that the Christian life finds its fullest expression in the corporate fellowship of the church. The Spirit manifests His presence through song, which enables one to express the melody of the heart to the Lord. In song, word, and deed, the Spirit-filled life is one of continual thanksgiving (5:20). When we begin to comprehend the grace of God made available in Christ, every circumstance leads to gratitude, which finds outward expression in praise.

This present section concludes with an exhortation to mutual subjection in the fear of Christ. This will be applied to various family and community relationships in the next section. Mutual subjection overcomes pride of position and an authoritarian spirit, which are destructive to fellowship. The Christian should manifest a humble spirit that is demonstrated by the willingness to serve anyone and learn from anyone in the fellowship. This may be a good time for a personal checkup concerning our willingness to learn from and serve others.

FOR MEMORY AND MEDITATION

"Therefore be imitators of God, as beloved children." Ephesians 5:1

Christ and His Church/ Husbands and Wives

CHAPTER 10

Focal Text: Ephesians 5:22–33

"These are challenging days for the church!" In my position as director of the Church Planting and Revitalization Center at North Greenville University, I hear this comment with increasing regularity. Sometimes it is from pastors who are embroiled in challenges and controversy that come because of changes happening in the church and the community around the church. Often it is from laypersons now aware that their church has been declining for years and is fighting for survival. They want their church to survive and thrive, but they are struggling to embrace the reality of the change that must occur and the hard work it will require. Some statisticians estimate that 80 percent of American churches are plateaued or declining.

These are also challenging days for the family! The traditional family is under attack. The attempts to redefine the family are becoming more and more confusing as the media provides multiple examples of the "new" family. But the challenges for the average family are much more personal than simply an overt attack on family values. The pace of life, finances, and the desire for more has challenged traditional roles and values in the Christian family.

As you read our focal text, you may be constantly wondering, Is Paul talking about the church or the family? The answer is both. The family and the church are intertwined, and the health and vitality of one will impact the other.

The Submission of Wives and the Church (5:22–24)

The word "submission" seems strangely out-of-date in a culture more intent on affirming one's rights than one's responsibilities. The words "be subject" are not found in verse 22 but must be supplied from verse 21, indicating that Paul is fleshing out what it means for believers to live "subject to one another in the fear of Christ." The submission of wives to their husbands is thus one particular expression of the submission all Christians must demonstrate in their relationship with others. We often are quick to forget that Christian living is about serving rather than being served.

A wife's submission to her husband is "as to the Lord." This does not mean she is to yield to him as she does to the Lord, for such would be idolatry. It means her submission to her husband is a duty she owes to the Lord. Thus submission does not suggest physical, mental, or spiritual inferiority. Throughout this section husbands and wives are reminded of their duties and not their rights. The husband's role is the more challenging and demanding, for he is required to love his wife the way Christ loved the church, giving Himself up for her (v. 25). The wife, in turn, joyfully submits to such leadership.

The New Testament emphasizes the dignity of womanhood. Historically, when the gospel penetrates any culture, the position of women has greatly improved. Men and women are declared to have spiritual equality (Gal. 3:28). Nonetheless, for the stability and unity of the family, sacrificial leadership and heavy responsibility fall to the husband.

Notice that Paul cannot discuss the role of the woman's submission without speaking of the husband's headship (v. 23). While the man's place is leadership, it is leadership qualified by self-giving love. Paul will devote the majority of the discussion to the role of the husband because his role demands the greatest sacrifice. As Christ is the Deliverer and Defender of the church, so the husband is the protector of his wife. If you think the submissive role of the wife seems foreign to our ears, the idea that the husband was to exercise sacrificial and self-giving leadership would have been strange to the ears of first-century readers.

In earlier Ephesian passages Paul has already used images of body and head (1:22–23) and temple and foundation (3:20–21) to illustrate the relationship of the church to Christ. But none of the images are as personal and intimate as that of husband and wife employed here. This image was frequently used in the Old Testament to describe Israel's relationship to God. God was spoken of as Husband of His people. He entered into a marriage relationship with them and thus loved them with a steadfast love. Israel's unfaithfulness could be compared to adultery. When we treat the church with casual disdain, we ignore the intimate love Christ has for His bride.

In verse 24, Paul returns to the matter of wifely submission, which takes its unique character from the special relationship which binds the Christian husband and wife. Genesis 2:4 will not be quoted until verse 31, but it governs this entire discussion. It is the sacrificial "leaving" and "cleaving" of the husband that creates a one-flesh bond. It is analogous to the supernatural relationship by which Christ is bound to His church. He left the glory of heaven to give Himself for His bride. The church/wife thus submits to the one who has given himself for her.

The phrase "in everything" (v. 24) does not mean the wife casts herself into the hands of one who has authority to command what he pleases even if it is wrong, oppressive, or abusive. She is to be submissive to one whose leadership is expressed by self-giving love, which places her needs first.

The Sacrificial Love of Husbands and Christ (5:25–31)

The husband's leadership is based on love, but it is not mere natural affection or sexual attraction. His love is agape love, which has been most clearly demonstrated by Christ who gave Himself up for the church. Agape love is totally unselfish. It is unceasing and self-sacrificing. It never seeks its own satisfaction but strives only for the highest good of the one loved. F. F. Bruce notes, "By setting this highest of standards for the husband's treatment of his wife, Paul goes to the limit in safeguarding the wife's dignity and welfare."[1] Husbands are never to think of what they expect in return for their love, but of what they may give from an unalloyed love.

As you read verses 26–27, notice that Paul's passionate concern in this letter is for the church, and thus he quickly leaves the conversation of husband and wife to focus again on the church. Christ's redemptive work was to set apart the church on earth as His unique possession. He gave Himself to sanctify and cleanse her (v. 26). The verb translated "sanctify" is aorist, indicating a single act. Christ sanctifies the church by cleansing her with "the washing of water with the word."

The "washing of water" would have surely called to mind baptism, but it must never be understood in terms of baptismal regeneration. The New Testament never suggests that any external act is sufficient to or necessary for salvation. Regeneration is an inward action of the Spirit which is symbolized by the outward act of baptism. "The word" probably means the gospel, which must be declared and verbally confessed. We see a similar pattern in Romans 10:8–10. Verse 8 speaks of the "word of faith" which was being preached, and verses 9–10 speak of belief and confession of that word which results in salvation.

Verse 27 causes us to think of the elaborate preparations the bride makes for her marriage that she may appear before her groom in all her beauty and holiness. The desire of the bride is to have neither spot nor wrinkle. Note that the beautifying treatment, in the case of the church, is the work of the groom and not the bride or her wedding party. The redemptive/sanctifying work of Christ allows the church to appear before Him in heaven in her perfected glory. The church, seen in our present experience, often falls fall short of the ideal. Thus the realization of God's great love for His now imperfect bride should create in us a passion to live up to our high calling (cf. Eph. 1:14).

Once again in verse 28, Paul returns to his discussion of the husband's love for his wife, which must be modeled on Christ's love for His church. The husband does not love his wife for the beauty he finds present in her but to bring forth her hidden beauty. His love will both nourish and cherish the loved one (v. 29). The statement that the husband is to love his wife as he loves himself cannot be misunderstood as suggesting that his love is merely an extension of his self-love designed to gain personal advantage for himself. The comparison with the self-giving love of Christ simply will not permit such a misunderstanding of this verse.

In order for a man to seek his own greatest spiritual welfare, he must seek first the highest good for his wife in every way. No one hates his own flesh, and since a man's wife is one flesh with him, the husband must love his wife to properly love himself. F. F. Bruce comments that when a man treats his wife as slave or chattel, it does as much to damage his own personality as it does to hers.[2] A man who fails to cherish and nourish his own wife lives a divided or schizophrenic spiritual existence. One must wonder if the lack of self-giving love among men may account for the disturbing lack of spiritual leadership in the home and the church.

Once again Paul admits he is still thinking primarily about the church (v. 29b). The exalted Christ has gifted (4:7–10) His church with everything necessary for her sustenance. And we must not forget that every believer is a member of His body (5:30). We are reminded that Paul would never countenance that any true follower of Christ could ever manifest a lack of nourishing and cherishing love for Christ's bride, the church. The general lack of attendance, participation, and giving to and through the church today makes one wonder if there is not a direct connection between the lack of spiritual leadership in the home and apathy toward the church.

The concluding thought of verse 31 is a quotation of Genesis 2:24. Jesus used these same words in Mark 10:7 to counsel against the casual nature with which some in His day treated divorce. Jesus recognized the possibility of divorce because of the hardness of men's hearts, but decreed that God's perfect plan in marriage was for one man and one woman for life. Here Paul quotes Genesis 2:24 to underline the vital unity which the marriage vow creates and to underline the necessity of sacrificial leadership of the husband. He is the one required to leave his home and cleave to his wife. Prior to marriage a man's closest bond is with his parents whom he must obey, but this new bond transcends the old. While Paul's primary concern throughout this passage is with Christ and His church, he sees throughout a parallel with the marriage relationship. Christ's self-giving love becomes the model for the man's leadership in the home and thus the glue that will enable a wife to submit joyfully and the children to obey without being provoked to anger (6:4).

The Great Mystery (5:32–33)

We are constantly reminded that Paul's preoccupation is with the church. Paul has used the word "mystery" on several earlier occasions (1:9; 3:3, 9; 6:19) to speak of the eternal secret of God's purpose for mankind. In 3:9 that mystery involved the church, which is to be the vessel through which God's manifold wisdom is revealed. Here "mystery" is used in the singular to speak of one particular truth of that divine plan. Marriage, rightly understood, can offer a picture of God's care for His church and the church's response to her Lord and Husband. The husband's sacrificial love and devoted care for his wife offer pictures, imperfect as they may be, of Christ's love and concern for His church. The dependence of the wife on her husband and her response of submission are a picture of how the church should live in relationship to the Lord.

Paul offers a final practical word about marriage that summarizes all that goes before. The husband's duty is one of self-giving love. The wife is to respect her husband, a respect earned by his self-giving love. The pattern is clear. The self-giving love of God birthed in us a desire to respond to Christ in submission. For a wife to reverence her husband, he has a Christlike mandate to earn her respect by sacrificial love.

This text will not allow us to ignore either the home or the church if we are to have a healthy society. Do a little spiritual check up. Does your involvement in your church demonstrate a self giving love? Do the relationships in your home model the image of Christ and His church?

FOR MEMORY AND MEDITATION

"Husbands, love your wives, just as Christ also loved the church and gave Himself up for her." Ephesians 5:25

---

[1] F. F. Bruce, *The Epistle to the Ephesians* (London: Pickering & Inglis LTD, 1961), 115.
[2] Ibid, 118.

Family Relationships

Focal Text: Ephesians 6:1–9

I was walking down the aisle of the church toward the balcony. The tiny voice of my youngest daughter, Katie, penetrated the nearly empty sanctuary. She first uttered a word that always melted my heart—"Daddy." I looked up and had two conflicting thoughts: "she knows that young children are not allowed in the balcony alone," and, "she is really cute". When she finished her statement, the first thought clearly won the battle. "Daddy, your bald spot is really big from up here!" At that moment I thought about the instruction to pastors that they must keep their children under control "with all dignity" (1 Tim. 3:4). How could I respond "with dignity" to such a cutie who was breaking the rules and reminding me of my growing bald spot?

Parenting is not for the timid. Parents are called to one of the most difficult of all tasks and often given little guidance in how to proceed. Children aren't born with a simple set of instructions. Even if they were, each one is so unique the instructions would have to be modified for each child. Paul follows the discussion of husband and wife with that of other relationships in the home. We need to be reminded that our discussion is still governed by the idea of mutual submission first mentioned in 5:21.

Children, Obey Your Parents (6:1–3)

Paul begins by calling children to the submissive act of obedience as he does in the parallel passage in Colossians 3:20. Once again this obedience is not unrestricted or blind obedience; it is modified by the phrase "in the Lord." Thus the context is clearly that of the Christian home where the parents embrace their role of discipline that involves "instruction of the Lord" (6:4). Paul does not address the context of a home where orders might be given which would be contrary to the law of Christ. The child's obedience to Christian parents who provide "instruction of the Lord" is analogous to the wife's submission to the self-giving love of the husband. Both the obedience of the child and the submission of the wife are the appropriate response to godly headship.

The context of the child's obedience is "in the Lord," which indicates it is a responsibility he/she owes to the Lord. The reason for the obedience is strikingly simple—"for this is right." This has been variously interpreted to mean right in every society, right based on Old Testament law, or right in accordance with the example of Christ. Luke, the only gospel writer to include a story of Jesus' childhood years, tells us that Jesus returned with His earthly parents from Jerusalem and "He continued in subjection to them" (Luke 2:51). Some commentators suggest that the phrase "for this is right" means children must trust their parents to such an extent that they obey before they can actually comprehend all the reasons for obedience. This is certainly true for young children.

While all of the above reasons for obedience may be implied in the simple phrase "for this is right," the Old Testament clearly teaches the need for children to honor/obey their parents. Jewish children would have been taught this commandment from birth and would have it indelibly imprinted in their memory. Paul now cites the fifth commandment, which deals with parents and children and indicates that it is the first commandment with a promise. In truth, it is the only commandment followed by a promise.

In verse 3, Paul quotes the promise attached to this commandment. Exodus 20:12 reads, "That your days may be prolonged in the land which the LORD your God gives you." The second statement of the law in Deuteronomy 5:16 reads, "That your days may be prolonged and that it may go well with you on the land which the LORD your God gives you." You may have noticed that the phrase "on the earth" replaces the idea of "the land which the Lord your God gives you." In the New Testament era, one would expect this natural transition from the idea of a physical promised land to that of one's earthly existence.

It is neither necessary nor likely that this promise was ever intended to be taken as a literal promise of personal and individual longevity. We think more individually than did the Israelites, who thought of themselves corporately as the people of God. Long life in the land of promise was the reward for keeping God's law in general and this law in particular. We should understand "long life" more in terms of the stability of the community and nation, which would result from the training of the children to obey God's law. When children fail to respect and obey their parents, the bonds of family life are destroyed, and the community or nation will soon become decedent. It will not long survive this downward spiral.

Paul had written earlier about disobedience to parents as one of the signs of the dissolution of society—"slanderers, haters of God, insolent, arrogant, boastful, inventors of evil, disobedient to parents" (Rom. 1:30). If you read this passage in its original context, you will find that it is found in a long list of despicable behaviors that are the result of the depraved mind (Rom. 1:28). We are so accustomed to disobedience that we think it somewhat harsh to put this minor offense in such a rogues' gallery of depraved behavior. Later in 2 Timothy 3:3, Paul lists disobedience to parents as one of the difficulties of the last days. Clearly this is an issue which must be clearly addressed by the church and the Christian family in our day.

Parents, Discipline Your Children (6:4)

The word for "fathers" is plural and should probably be translated as "parents." For children to joyfully obey their parents, parents must discipline and instruct in such a way that children desire to obey. Paul begins by warning that parents must not provoke their children to anger. The word is a present active imperative implying unreasonable demands that lead one to a deep-seated anger. It is appropriate that parents should expect their children to obey, but they cannot lead in a cruel and capricious way that will cause children to wonder if it is possible ever to please their parents. In Colossians, the companion letter to Ephesians, Paul writes: "Fathers, do not exasperate your children, so that they will not lose heart" (3:21).

The dictatorial model of parenting, which is often punctuated with the phrase "because I said so," must be replaced with one which focuses on discipline and instruction. The word translated "bring up" is the same word used in 5:29 for the husband nourishing his wife. Parents are to provide for the tender care of their children by providing both discipline and instruction. "Discipline" is used to speak of correcting the transgression of the laws and rules of the Christian household. The word translated "instruction" refers to training by the word. First it would be the word of encouragement and then, when necessary, the word of reproof and correction. Do you speak words of encouragement as well as words of reproof?

But the instruction in the Christian home is uniquely "instruction of the Lord." The issue is not merely harmony in the home, or the intellectual prowess of the child, or the worldly success of the child, but the issue is their relationship to the Lord and regard for His teachings. The Christian parent knows that the true happiness and success of their child flow from their growing relationship with Christ. Christian parents place the loyalty of their children to Christ above any other attainment.

I was privileged to grow up as a preacher's kid. As I look back on that experience, I appreciate that my father never disciplined me for behavior unbecoming a preacher's son. His discipline and instruction were always related to my personal relationship to Christ. I was held to the same standards he expected of any other believer in our church. Does your instruction to your children indicate that your greatest concern is for their spiritual growth? Do you ask them about their Bible study habits as often as you ask about their homework and grades? Does your personal instruction embody truths from Scripture?

Workers, Serve as Slaves of Christ (6:5–9)

In the culture of the first century, Paul would still be dealing with the family household setting. Many of the early followers of Christ were likely slaves. While we must first understand this in terms of the first century, the concepts taught here can be applied to employees and employers in our present-day context.

Once again we see a specific application of the principle of mutual submission. The word "obedient" is the same as that used in verse 1 in terms of the response of children to parents. The phrase "according to the flesh" is a poignant reminder that their present status is temporary since it belongs to the passing world order. Further, it reminds readers that they are servants of a higher Master.

A slave could have been a leader in the church because of his giftedness. A slave's obedience to his master would take on special significance when his master was also his brother in Christ. If a slave has a pagan master, he would desire to be a faithful servant for the sake of the gospel. His behavior could lead to the conversion of his earthly master.

The phrase "with fear and trembling" is similar to "in the fear of Christ" (5:21) and thus alerts us again that this entire section is about mutual submission in the body of Christ. The word "fear," which means "reverence," indicates that our relationship to Christ makes every relationship sacred. In the case of the slave or worker, his service to his earthly master is to be offered as if he is presenting it to the Lord. For the employee today it means that honesty and wholehearted effort must characterize the work of the Christian employee.

Verse 6 makes clear that the Christian cannot put on a show of hard work when being watched and then ignore his responsibility when no one is watching. We could understand how a slave could be less than committed to his task when he is serving against his will. It is more difficult to understand how a Christian, who has freely entered into a contract with his employer, could give less than his best when the reputation of Christ is at stake. The Christian has the highest possible reason for doing quality work since he is "doing the will of God from the heart" (v. 6).

The believer does his work with good will or a ready willingness because he knows he is presenting his labor to the Lord. Each day we should think that every task we complete should be good enough to present to the Lord. After all, the Lord will judge and thus reward all that is done, even that which is done in the marketplace. The "receiving back" for good work might happen, in part, while on earth, but Paul is thinking about the final reckoning and one's eternal reward. The fact that nothing goes unnoticed and unrewarded by the Lord in heaven is the only incentive necessary to motivate the Christian to do everything well. The final phrase of verse 8 makes clear that all believers, slave and free alike, are to present their labor to the Lord.

Masters, Do the Same Things (6:9)

Paul's instructions to the masters would have been radical for his day and time. He instructs masters to apply these principles of willing service "as unto the Lord" to themselves. They must view their work as one aspect of their total life stewardship. They must superintend their slaves without resorting to threats. In the context of slavery, the master could speak to or abuse a slave as he desired, and the slave would have no recourse. Employers today might feel they have absolute authority over their employees since they pay the bills, but nothing could be further from the truth for the Christian employer. Both employer and employee serve the same Master who judges without partiality.

This lesson may prompt us to question why no command was given to free all slaves. To have done so at this time in history would have confirmed the suspicion of those in authority that the Christian movement was aimed at the subversion of society. Under the inspiration of the Holy Spirit, Paul realized it was better to articulate the principles inherent in the gospel and allow them to have their impact in due course. In this verse are contained the seeds that would one day destroy the sinful institution of slavery.

FOR MEMORY AND MEDITATION
"Fathers, do not provoke your children to anger, but bring them up in the discipline and instruction of the Lord." Ephesians 6:4

Put On the Full Armor of God

CHAPTER 12

Focal Text: Ephesians 6:10–24

We may give lip service to the idea of spiritual warfare, but few of us take it seriously in our daily lives. We fall into the pattern of blaming our circumstances or other persons for our problems and our failures. We seldom think of struggling against world powers of darkness. We vilify other persons, treating them like our enemies, rather than reminding ourselves that we face a spiritual opponent who has come to steal, kill, and destroy.

I suppose some of us want to avoid the trap of seeing a demon behind every bush or even hiding in our washing machine when it fails to work. We have all experienced persons who blame the devil for everything and take little responsibility for their own actions. But such aberrant views should not cause us to ignore the clear teaching of Scripture concerning the spiritual conflict we face daily. Since we are engaged in a spiritual battle, we need to understand fully the resources given to us by our exalted Lord.

A Call to Arms (6:10–13)

An exhortation to manifest spiritual strength is common in the New Testament. Earlier in Ephesians 1:19, Paul prayed that his readers would know the "surpassing greatness of His power toward us who believe." This power available to believers is the same power God exerted in raising His Son from the dead. In Ephesians 3:16, Paul prayed that believers would be

101

"strengthened with power through His Spirit in the inner man." This inner strength is an enduring supernatural strength, which is the essential element of spiritual victory.

We should not overlook the truth that our strength is "the strength of His might," or "His mighty strength." This call to arms is a fitting end to this letter which began with a listing of all the spiritual blessings found in Christ. Our strength is based on the victory established by the crucifixion and resurrection of Christ. By virtue of our incorporation into Christ, we have been raised and enthroned with Him in the heavenly places. Thus we do not simply strive for victory; we live from the position of victory already won.

For maximum impact we must pay close attention to the immediate context. From chapter 4 onwards Paul has been dealing with the issue of living and ministering in church, community, and family. In our church, our family life, and our marketplace relationships, the spiritual battle becomes most intense. The life to which the believer is called cannot be lived without encountering spiritual conflict. Thus Paul begins with the present passive "be strong," which could be better translated "be continually made strong." Believers cannot strengthen themselves, for our strength is "in the Lord."

We must not fight spiritual battles without God's strength or His armor. Paul will return to the matter of armor later in this passage and describe the pieces in detail, but at this point he reminds the readers that believers can only win against the devil's schemes when we are clothed in God's armor. The armor is both that which God wears (see the description of the heavenly warrior in Isa. 59:17) and that which He provides to His followers.

"The schemes of the devil" (6:11) are the strategies he employs to gain advantage over God's people. This same word is used in Ephesians 4:14 where the issue was doctrinal error. Satan can put obstacles in our way (1 Thess. 2:18), exploit human relationships (1 Cor. 7:5), even take the form of an angel of light (2 Cor. 11:3, 14), but his work will always be cloaked in deceit. The believer's response to such deceptive power is to "stand firm." We hold the fortress for the heavenly King as we stand in doctrinal integrity with the full armor and army of God. We are foolish to think we can stand against the devil without the full covering of the church and its gifted leaders (4:11–14).

While talk of a personal devil may seem quaint and out-of-date to some today, we would be foolish to think ourselves wiser than our Lord and the early apostles concerning the reality of the unseen world. The word "struggle" (6:12) conveys the personal and individual nature of spiritual warfare, which often takes the form of hand-to-hand combat. The terms "rulers," "powers," "world forces of this darkness," and "spiritual forces of wickedness" remind us of the similar list in 1:21. Paul is saying that whatever spiritual powers exists and by whatever name one calls those powers, all have been conquered by Christ through the resurrection when He stripped them of their armor and He drove them before Him in triumphal procession (Col. 2:15; cf. Eph. 4:8–10).

The present world order is described as being

under the control of darkness (6:12). The ultimate doom of Satan and his demons has been sealed; yet in the overlap of the ages, they continue to exercise influence and control over all who do not avail themselves of the way of release from their dominion. Only in Christ can men be released from Satan's grasp and gain daily victory over him (cf. 1 John 5:19). By virtue of our personal relationship with Christ, we have already been raised up with Him and seated in the heavenly places (Eph. 2:1–6). The adversary and his minions want to rob us of our spiritual position and our spiritual possessions.

We can be assured that, as we take up the full armor of God, we will be able "to resist in the evil day" and "to stand firm" (6:13). The "evil day" describes the present age as in Ephesians 5:16. It is evil because the vanquished evil forces are still able to exercise control over those who do not stand in Christ's victory and don God's armor. When we find ourselves caught up in circumstances and behavior patterns we cannot control, we may feel like helpless victims of "blind fate." Our enemy is not blind fate but a personal adversary. We cannot win this spiritual battle by the strength of our might but only by "the strength of His might" (v. 10) and only clothed with His armor. Our role is not to fight but to stand—to stand in Christ's victory.

The Armor Described (6:14–17)

Paul may have based the detailed description of armor in this passage on the Roman soldier who guarded him as he wrote from prison. We have both defensive armor and offensive weapons for our spiritual battle. The defensive pieces of armor are similar to the fruit of the Spirit as described in Galatians 5:22–24. The armor is described based on the order in which a soldier would put it on.

The girdle is not armor in the strictest sense, but girding describes the actual process of the binding together of the undergarments as a foundation for putting on the armor. The idea of "girding the loins" is often used in the Bible as a necessary preparatory action before work could be done or a race run. Our girdle is "truth," which includes loyalty and faithfulness. Paul is speaking of the integrity of one's spiritual life. It must be based on the truth of God's word.

The "breastplate of righteousness" may refer both to the righteousness that comes from Christ—our new standing in Him—and the righteousness that is a result of character and practice. Isaiah, speaking of the coming Messiah, declares, "He put on righteousness like a breastplate" (59:17a). When we neglect to live righteously, we leave a gaping hole in our armor. If you have read John Bunyan's Pilgrim's Progress, you may remember that Pilgrim's armor included no protection for the back, requiring him to face his foe.

Scholars debate whether the footwear—"the gospel of peace"—is related to declaring the gospel (evangelism) or standing firm based on one's absolute confidence in the gospel. I think it is likely a reference to both since sandals allow the soldier to stand firm and to advance. The defensive role of the sandals would depend on the truth of the gospel—one's assurance of salvation—which gives one peace in his heart, allowing him to stand firm in the midst of spiritual conflict. If Isaiah 52:7 is in mind ("How lovely on the mountains are the feet of him who brings good news"), we can hardly neglect the necessity for the soldier to declare the good news. Even in the midst of a spiritual war, the Christian is the messenger of peace.

The phrase translated "in addition to all" could well be understood as "to cover all the rest." Paul has in mind the large body shield, which could cover the entire body of the soldier. "Faith" refers to one's total reliance on God. When Jesus was tested by the devil (Matt. 4), He extinguished all of Satan's accusations by His absolute trust in God, requiring no outward sign or additional proof. The shield of faith will "extinguish all the flaming arrows of the evil one" (v. 16). In ancient times arrows were dipped in pitch and set on fire before they were launched. A wooden shield had to be covered in leather to quench the fire. The flaming arrows of the adversary may be shafts of disappointment, self-doubt, fear, impurity, or even the accusations of men. Our total reliance on God alone can extinguish all these flaming arrows.

After putting on his armor, the soldier takes up the helmet of salvation. God's gift of salvation not only saves us from the penalty of sin; it also protects us from the power of sin and assures us that one day we will be saved from the presence of sin. In other words, we will win this battle with the adversary.

Finally, we take up "the sword of the Spirit" (v. 17). In the Old Testament "sword" is often used to refer to speech or words. For example, the psalmist says that the words of wicked men wound like a sword (57:4). The sword we wield is "the sword of the Spirit." The

Spirit puts it in our grasp and empowers its use. We should be reminded of our Lord's use of Scripture when He was under attack by the adversary (Matt. 4). The sword can be used against the adversary and for the benefit of others as it provides an utterance appropriate to the occasion. This is the only offensive weapon the soldier carries, but it is all he needs, for it is invincible. God's word "is living and active and sharper than any two-edged sword" (Heb. 4:12), and it always accomplishes its purpose (Isa. 55:11).

Covered with Prayer (6:18–20)

As you read verse 18, notice the fourfold repetition of "all." This verse is a poignant reminder that even a fully armed soldier will be defeated if he/she is not covered with prayer. Further, we are reminded that we stand side by side with "all the saints" in this spiritual conflict. We cannot go into battle without growing closer to those who join us in that battle. The linking of "prayer" and "petition" adds intensity to the call for prayer. "At all times" reminds us that prayer is not just for the difficult moments when we fear defeat. Prayer is the default setting of our life since we are dependent every moment on Gods' grace and power. The Spirit has many roles as our "helper," and one of the most critical has to do with prayer (Rom. 8:26). The call to watchfulness and persistence reminds us of our Lord's parable in Luke 18.

Paul, living in house arrest with a chain around his wrist which handcuffed him to the Roman soldier who guarded him, felt the need for prayer. Notice that he doesn't ask his readers to pray for the alteration of his circumstances but for advancement of the gospel. Paul asks for boldness and clarity as he proclaimed "the mystery of the gospel." The gospel, which in times past was kept secret, has now been made clear in Christ (cf. Rom. 16:25). Many ambassadors came to Rome, but none were more important than this diminutive man chained to a Roman soldier, for he was called to represent the King of kings (cf. 2 Cor. 5:20).

Paul's Circumstances (6:21–22)

Paul shares a few details of his present circumstances so his readers can be better informed in their praying. Tychicus, the bearer of this letter, Colossians (see 4:7), and the Philemon letter will provide additional information when he arrives. Tychicus is described as a brother and faithful minister of the Lord. Tychicus was a delegate of the Gentile churches who accompanied Paul to Judaea in AD 57 to provide relief to the saints in Jerusalem. One might expect a prisoner to seek comfort from others, but the great apostle wants to comfort the hearts of those who will be praying for him.

A Final Benediction (6:23–24)

The general nature of the benediction further indicates the wider audience for which this letter was intended. Paul's three blessings (peace, love, and grace) have been the consistent focus of this letter. Paul desires that his readers experience peace with God and with one another and love that springs from faithfulness. These blessings, as in Ephesians 1:3, come from God who is the Mediator of every spiritual blessing. The final prayer is for grace for those who love the

Lord with incorruptible or undying love. Love is incorruptible because it is eternal in nature. "But now faith, hope, love, abide these three; but the greatest of these is love" (1 Cor. 13:13).

FOR MEMORY AND MEDITATION

"Put on the full armor of God, so that you will be able to stand firm against the schemes of the devil." Ephesians 6:11

Appendix

The promises of this book are based on one's relationship to Christ. If you have not yet entered a personal relationship with Jesus Christ, I encourage you to make this wonderful discovery today. I like to use the very simple acrostic—LIFE—to explain this, knowing that God wants you not only to inherit *eternal* life but also to experience *earthly* life to its fullest.

L = Love

It all begins with God's Love. God created you in his image. This means you were created to live in relationship with him. *"For God loved the world in this way: He gave His One and Only Son, so that everyone who believes in Him will Not perish but have eternal life"* (John 3:16).

But if God loves you and desires a relationship with you, why do you feel so isolated from Him?

I = Isolation

This isolation is created by our sin—our rebellion against God—which separates us from him and from others. *"For all have sinned and fall short of the glory of God"* (Romans 3:23). *"For the wages of sin is death, but the gift of God is eternal life in Christ Jesus our Lord"* (Romans 6:23).

You might wonder how you can overcome this isolation and have an intimate relationship with God.

F = Forgiveness

The only solution to man's isolation and separation from a holy God is forgiveness. *"For Christ also suffered for sins once and for all, the righteous for the unrighteous, that He might bring you to God, after being put to death in the fleshly realm but made alive in the spiritual realm"* (1 Peter 3:18).

The only way our relationship can be restored with God is through the forgiveness of our sins. Jesus Christ died on the cross for this very purpose.

E = Eternal Life

You can have a full and abundant life in this present life… and eternal life when you die. *"But to all who did receive Him, He gave them the right to be children of God, to those who believe His name"* (John 1:12). *"A thief comes only to steal and to kill and to destroy. I have come that they may have life and have it in abundance"* (John 10:10).

Is there any reason you wouldn't like to have a personal relationship with God?

THE PLAN OF SALVATION

It's as simple as ABC. All you have to do is:

A = Admit you are a sinner. Turn from your sin and turn to God. *"Repent and turn back, that your sins may be wiped out so that seasons of refreshing may come from the presence of the Lord"* (Acts 3:19).

B = Believe that Jesus died for your sins and rose from the dead enabling you to have life. *"I have written these things to you who believe in the name of the Son of God, so that you may know that you have eternal life"* (1 John 5:13).

C = Confess verbally and publicly your belief in Jesus Christ. *"If you confess with your mouth, 'Jesus is Lord,' and believe in your heart that God raised Him from the dead, you will be saved. With the heart one believes, resulting in righteousness, and with the mouth one confesses, resulting in salvation"* (Rom. 10:9–10).

You can invite Jesus Christ to come into your life right now. Pray something like this:

"God, I admit that I am a sinner. I believe that you sent Jesus, who died on the cross and rose from the dead, paying the penalty for my sins. I am asking that you forgive me of my sin, and I receive your gift of eternal life. It is in Jesus' name that I ask for this gift. Amen."

Signed _____

Date _____

If you have a friend or family member who is a Christian, tell them about your decision. Then find a church that teaches the Bible, and let them help you go deeper with Christ.

Free teaching guides

for all non-disposable curricula
for 12- or 13-week study
are available at

www.auxanopress.com

Audio commentary by the
author and "Good Questions" by
Josh Hunt are available for most
studies at a small additional cost.

Non-Disposable Curriculum

• Study the Bible and build a Christian library!
• Designed for use in any small group.
• Affordable, biblically based, and life oriented.
• Free teaching helps and administrative materials online.
• Choose your own material and stop/start time.

Audio-commentary material for teachers by the author at additional cost.

Other Volumes Available Now

Core Convictions: Confidence About What You Believe
When people have confidence about what they believe, they are more inclined to make daily decisions from a Biblical perspective. Ken Hemphill

Connected Community: Becoming Family Through Church
Only the church can deliver authentic community that will last forever. This study explores the mystery of God's eternal plan to reveal His manifold wisdom through the Church.
Ken Hemphill

God's Redemption Story: Old Testament Survey
Explores the story line of the Old Testament by focusing on twelve key events in the life of Israel and linking them together to provide a unified view of God's redemptive work in history. Ken Hemphill

The King and His Community: New Testament Survey
Begins with the birth of Jesus and ends with Him walking among the seven churches of the book of Revelation. It covers key passages that tell the story of the King and the worldwide spread of His church. Kie Bowman